**Que® Quick Reference Series**

# dBASE IV® Quick Reference

Deborah L. Stone

Que® Corporation
Carmel, Indiana

Library of Congress Catalog No.:  88-61930

ISBN 0-88022-371-5

92  91  90 89                  4   3   2   1

Interpretation of the printing code:  the rightmost
double-digit number is the year of the book's printing;
the rightmost single-digit number, the number of the
book's printing.  For example, a printing code of 87-4
shows that the fourth printing of the book occurred in
1987.  .

Based on dBASE IV Release 1.0 and the earlier release
dBASE III Plus.

# Que Quick Reference Series

The *Que Quick Reference Series* is a portable resource
of essential microcomputer knowledge. Whether you
are a new or experienced user, you can rely on the high-
quality information contained in these convenient
guides.

Drawing on the experience of many of Que's best-
selling authors, the *Que Quick Reference Series* helps
you easily access important program information.
Now it's easy to look up often-used commands and
functions for 1-2-3, WordPerfect 5, MS-DOS, and
dBASE IV, as well as programming information for
Assembly Language, C and QuickBASIC 4.

Use the *Que Quick Reference Series* as a compact
alternative to confusing and complicated traditional
documentation.

The *Que Quick Reference Series* also includes these
titles:

> *1-2-3 Quick Reference*
> *Assembly Language Quick Reference*
> *C Quick Reference*
> *DOS and BIOS Functions Quick Reference*
> *Hard Disk Quick Reference*
> *MS-DOS Quick Reference*
> *QuickBASIC Quick Reference*
> *WordPerfect Quick Reference*

### *Trademark Acknowledgments*
- dBASE IV, dBASE III Plus, and dBASE II are
  registered trademarks of Ashton-Tate Company.
- Macintosh is a registered trademark of Apple
  Computer, Inc.
- MS-DOS is a registered trademark of Microsoft
  Corporation.
- PageMaker is a registered trademark of Aldus
  Corporation.

# TABLE OF CONTENTS

# dBASE IV Command Reference

Each dBASE IV command is presented in the same format: the purpose appears first, followed by reminders, proper syntax, step-by-step procedures, and a "notes" section containing additional comments and hints. Cautions are given for some commands.

In the statement of syntax, the command appears in all uppercase and in blue—**COMMAND**. Variable information appears in lowercase italic enclosed in angle brackets—*<information>*. Do not type the brackets when you enter the information. Optional interior commands appear in uppercase enclosed in brackets—[COMMAND]. Do not type the brackets when you enter the command.

See **STORE**

# ?, ??, ???

### *Purpose*

Displays information on your screen or printer with the ?, ?? commands. Sends special codes to the printer with the ??? command.

### *Reminder*

Include the CHR( ) function in the ??? command line.

### *Command Syntax*

?/?? [*<expression-1>* [PICTURE "*<clause>*"]
[FUNCTION "*<function-list>*"] [AT *<expN>*]
[STYLE *<font-number>*]] [,*<expression-2>*,...]

??? *<control-character>*

## Procedures

### From the Dot Prompt:

1.  Issue the ? command when you need to display an
    expression or value on the next line. The ??
    command displays the expression without
    advancing to the next line.
2.  Send printer commands without moving the print
    head with the ??? commands. The following
    commands are for an EPSON printer. Check your
    printer manual for the correct font codes.

```
??? chr(15)
? "Test of condensed print."
STYLE "B"
??? chr(18)
? "Back to normal size." STYLE "I"
```

### From the Control Center:

No equivalent menu options are in the Control Center.

## Notes

Control the style of output with STYLE. Enclose any
style options in double quotes. The style options are
Bold, Subscript, Underline, Italic, and Superscript (B, L,
U, I, and R).

Control the format of output with the following
functions:

| | |
|---|---|
| H $<n>$ | Stretch a field horizontally a maximum $n$ columns. |
| V $<n>$ | Stretch a field vertically a maximum $n$ rows. |
| B | Left-aligns text within a field. |
| I | Centers text within a field. |
| J | Right-aligns text within a field. |
| T | Trims leading and trailing blanks. |
| $ | Displays a floating currency symbol before or after a numeric field. The position of the symbol is controlled with SET CURRENCY LEFT or RIGHT. |
| L | Displays numeric fields with leading zeros. |

See **RUN**

See **NOTE**

# @..SAY, GET

### Purpose

Positions the cursor or information on the screen or printer page.

### Reminder

Most monitors have 24 lines down and 80 columns across. An 8 1/2 by 11 inch page allows 66 lines down and 80 columns across in normal print font and 75 lines down and 132 columns across in condensed font.

### Command Syntax

@ *<row>,<col>* [SAY *<expression>* [PICTURE "*<clause>*"] [FUNCTION "*<function-list>*"]] [GET *<variable>* [[OPEN] WINDOW *<window-name>*] [PICTURE "*<clause>*"] [FUNCTION "*<function-list>*"] [RANGE *<low>*, *<high>*] [VALID *<condition>*] [ERROR *<expC>*]] [WHEN *<condition>*] [DEFAULT *<expression>*] [MESSAGE *<expC>*]] [COLOR [*<standard>*] [,*<enhanced>*]]

**READ** [SAVE]

### Procedures

#### From the Dot Prompt:

1. Use the @..SAY command to position and display

screen and printer information. A SET DEVICE TO
PRINTER command causes all following @..SAY
commands to be sent to the printer. SET DEVICE
TO SCREEN redirects @..SAY commands back to
the screen.

2. The @..GET command specifies an input area for
   user input. Restrict the size and type of input with
   the PICTURE clause.

3. Use the DEFAULT option to suggest a preset
   value for a @..GET.

4. Use the ERROR option to specify your custom
   error message. The default error message is
   "Editing condition not satisfied."

***From the Control Center:***

Create a screen or report form to position information.

### Notes

A single READ command obtains data from a screenful
of @..GET commands. The READ command is required
to activate the @..GET commands. The program stops
and waits for the user to fill or pass all input areas before
resuming.

Line 22 is unavailable for your use if SET STATUS is
set to ON. Line 0 is unavailable for your use if SET
SCOREBOARD is set to ON.

### Caution

Remember to redirect output back to the screen with the
SET DEVICE TO SCREEN command after a SET
DEVICE TO PRINT command, or screen information
will be sent to the printer.

# @...TO, FILL, CLEAR

### Purpose

Outlines, colors, or clears areas on the screen. Use this
technique to customize screen appearance.

## Reminder

These commands overlay information already on your screen.

## Command Syntax

@ <row-1>,<col-1> **TO** <row-2>,<col-2>
[DOUBLE/PANEL/<border-definition-string>] [COLOR <color-attribute>]

@ <row-1>,<col-1> **FILL TO** <row-2>,<col-2>
[COLOR <color-attribute>]

@ <row-1>,<col-1> **CLEAR** [TO <row-2>,<col-2>]

## Procedures

### From the Dot Prompt:

The following commands draw and fill a box on the screen:

```
@ 08,15 to 14,60 double color r/w
@ 09,16 fill to 13,59 color w/n
```

### From the Control Center:

1. Select the Create option from the Forms column of the Control Center.
2. Select the Layout/Box/Double options to draw a double line box.
3. Anchor the upper left corner of the box by positioning the cursor at the desired location and pressing Enter. Stretch the box with the arrow keys and press Enter to complete it.
4. Press F6 to select the box.
5. Press F10. Then, select the Words/Display submenus. Use the arrow keys to move to the desired color and press Enter to select it. Do this for foreground as well as background colors. Press Ctrl-End to select the color combination and exit the submenus.

## Note

If you open multiple windows on a screen, consider offsetting or overlaying the preceding one.

## Caution

Avoid overlaying information that the user needs to keep on the screen.

# ACCEPT

## Purpose

Stops program activity and asks the user for information. For example, asks the user for a date range used when extracting data.

## Reminder

Use the ACCEPT command to create character or numeric data type variables.

## Command Syntax

ACCEPT [*<prompt>*] TO *<memvar>*

## Procedures

### From the Dot Prompt:

Issue the ACCEPT command from the dot prompt or in a program as in the following example:

```
ACCEPT "Enter the beginning date ";
TO MFROM
```

### From the Control Center:

There is no equivalent capability from the Control Center.

## Note

The INPUT and WAIT commands also stop program processing until the user responds.

*Caution*

When you use the ACCEPT, INPUT, or WAIT commands, you cannot control the user's response.

# ACTIVATE MENU

See **DEFINE MENU**

# ACTIVATE POPUP

See **DEFINE POPUP**

# ACTIVATE SCREEN

*Purpose*

Allows the entire screen to be used or active rather than a predefined window. Other windows may be scrolled or cleared from the screen.

*Reminder*

Identify the window to be opened on the screen.

*Command Syntax*

**ACTIVATE SCREEN**

*Procedures*

*From the Dot Prompt:*

Write a program and include a combination of the windowing command lines.

```
DEFINE WINDOW Test from 3,5 to 10,50
ACTIVATE WINDOW Test
    ? "This is the Active window."
ACTIVATE SCREEN
CLEAR
```

The ACTIVATE SCREEN command line causes the window to stretch and cover the whole screen.
*From the Control Center:*
There is no equivalent capability from the submenus.

*Notes*

Define and use windows to restrict the user's attention (and response) to a selected area of information.

Other window commands are the DEFINE WINDOW, ACTIVATE WINDOW, DEACTIVATE WINDOW, MOVE WINDOW, SAVE WINDOW, RESTORE WINDOW, and RELEASE WINDOW.

*Caution*

If you open too many windows on the screen at one time, you might confuse the user.

# ACTIVATE WINDOW

See **DEFINE WINDOW**

# APPEND

*Purpose*

Adds records to a dBASE IV datafile. Do this by typing new records from the keyboard.

*Reminder*

Use the PgUp and PgDn keys to move to the preceding and next record. End the append activity by pressing Ctrl-End.

*Command Syntax*
APPEND  [BLANK]

## *Procedures*

### *From the Dot Prompt:*

1. Open the datafile by issuing the USE command.
2. Type `APPEND` and press Enter. A blank record appears on your screen. This is called the Append Mode.
3. Type the data in each area of the blank record. When the record is filled, another blank record is made available.
4. Press Ctrl-End to exit Append Mode.

### *From the Control Center:*

1. Position the bounce bar on a file and press Enter to select it.
2. When asked, select the Modify Structure/Order option.
3. Use the arrow keys to open the Append submenu and select the Enter Records from Keyboard option to use the Append Mode.

## *Note*

All new records are added to the end of the datafile just like you would add to a paper list.

## *Caution*

Never turn off the machine while appending records to the datafile. Doing so is likely to damage the datafile so that you lose much of the data you have entered.

# APPEND FROM

## *Purpose*

Adds records to a database from an array or another database.

## *Reminder*

The array elements of information must be in the same order as the record structure. The first array element value is moved to the first field in the record, etc.

dBASE IV ignores extra array elements (length only). A record for each array is automatically added to the datafile.

*Command Syntax*

**APPEND FROM ARRAY** *<array-name>* [**FOR** *<condition>*]

**APPEND FROM** *<file-name>*/? [[TYPE] *<file-type>*] [**FOR** *<condition>*]

*Procedures*

*From the Dot Prompt:*

1. Before you use the APPEND FROM ARRAY command, make sure that the array has been declared and filled with information.
2. Issue the APPEND FROM command to get information from another file.

*From the Control Center:*

1. Position the bounce bar on a file and press Enter to select it.
2. When asked, select the Modify Structure/Order option.
3. Use the arrow keys to open the Append submenu and select an option.
4. Choose either Append Records from dBASE File or Copy Records from Non-dBASE File.

*Notes*

Valid *<file-types>* are DBASEII, DELIMITED, DELIMITED WITH, DIF (VisiCalc), FW2 (Framework II), RPD (RapidFile), SDF (System Data Format), SYLK (MultiPlan), WKS (Lotus 1-2-3).

Use the IMPORT command to convert the incoming file to a valid file type.

*Caution*

Blank rows in any spreadsheet file type are converted to blank records for the datafile.

# APPEND MEMO

### Purpose
Reads a file into the specified memo field of the open database.

### Reminder
The database must include a memo field before you issue this command.

### Command Syntax
**APPEND MEMO** *<memo-field-name>* **FROM** *<file-name>* [OVERWRITE]

### Procedures
**From the Dot Prompt:**
Include the OVERWRITE clause to replace the value of the specified memo field. Otherwise, the memo field value is extended with the new information.
**From the Control Center:**
1. Position the bounce bar on a file and press Enter to select it.
2. When asked, select the Modify Structure/Order option.
3. Use the arrow keys to open the Append submenu and select Enter Records from Keyboard.
4. Press Ctrl-Home to open the memo field.
5. Press F10 to access the menu and select Words/ Write/Read Text File/Read Text from the File.

### Caution
An error occurs if you specify a field that does not exist or is not a memo field.

# ASSIST

### Purpose

Accesses the dBASE IV Control Center screen rather than the dot prompt.

### Reminder

Use the Control Center screen by positioning the bounce bar on an option or file name and pressing Enter to select it.

### Command Syntax

ASSIST

### Procedures

1. From the dot prompt, type ASSIST or press F2.
2. Return to the dot prompt from the Control Center screen by pressing the Esc key and answer Yes to end the current operation.

### Note

Begin every session at the Control Center by changing the CONFIG.DB file. It must include the COMMAND= ASSIST command line. (This is a default line in the CONFIG.DB file when installed.)

### Caution

Several dot prompt capabilities are not available from the Control Center.

# AVERAGE

See CALCULATE

# BEGIN TRANS, END TRANS

## Purpose

Records changes to a database with the option to return back to the database's original state.

## Reminder

Each BEGIN TRANSACTION command line must have a matching END TRANSACTION command line.

## Command Syntax

BEGIN TRANSACTION [<*path-name*>]
  <*commands*>
END TRANSACTION

ROLLBACK [<*datafile-name*>]

## Procedures

### From the Dot Prompt:

1. Include the BEGIN TRANSACTION command to identify the starting point for transaction processing. The END TRANSACTION command marks the end.
2. Use the ROLLBACK command to abort the results of the command lines between the BEGIN TRANSACTION and END TRANSACTION.

### From the Control Center:

There is no equivalent method from the Control Center.

## Notes

Use the ROLLBACK command to restore the database file to its pretransaction state.

The ROLLBACK command is effective for the APPEND, BROWSE, CHANGE, DELETE, EDIT, RECALL, REPLACE, and UPDATE commands. Also, create new files by using the COPY, CREATE, IMPORT FROM, INDEX, JOIN, SET CATALOG, SORT, and TOTAL commands.

If you intend to use the rollback capability, you cannot close or overwrite any open files.

The RESET command line tags the files involved in transaction processing. It marks the file when processing begins and is removed upon completion of the procedure or when the ROLLBACK command is used.

*Caution*

Do not include the CLEAR ALL, CLOSE, DELETE FILE, ERASE, INSERT, MODIFY STRUCTURE, PACK, RENAME, or ZAP commands in transaction processing.

# BROWSE

*Purpose*

Allows viewing/changing the information in an existing datafile. Also, use this command to control modification of data.

*Reminder*

Use the following keys while using the Browse Mode:

| | |
|---|---|
| Ctrl-U | Flag or unflag a record for deletion |
| Ctrl-Q | End the edit session without saving the data changes |
| Ctrl-W | End the edit session and save the data changes |
| PgUp | Move to the previous screen |
| PgDn | Move to the next screen |
| Up arrow | Move to the previous field or record |
| Down arrow | Move to the next field or record |
| Right arrow | Move to the next character |
| Left arrow | Move to the previous character |
| Ctrl-Left arrow | Move to the next field |
| Ctrl-Right arrow | Move to the previous field |

## *Command Syntax*

**BROWSE** [NOINIT] [NOFOLLOW] [NOAPPEND]
[NOMENU] [NOEDIT] [NODELETE] [NOCLEAR]
[COMPRESS] [FORMAT] [LOCK *<expN>*]
[WIDTH *<expN>*] [FREEZE *<field-name>*]
[WINDOW *<window-name>*] [FIELDS *<field-name-
1>* [/R] [/*<column-width>*] /*<calculated-field-name-
1>* =*<expression-1>* [,*<field-name-2>* [/R]
[/*<column-width>*] /*<calculated-field-2>* =
*<expression-2>*] ...]

## *Procedures*

### *From the Dot Prompt:*

1. Open the file with the USE command.
2. Type BROWSE, select any desired options, and press Enter.
3. View and change any information in the database. Press Ctrl-W to save the changes and return to the dot prompt.
4. Close the open database by typing USE and pressing Enter.

### *From the Control Center:*

1. Position the bounce bar on the datafile name.
2. Press the F2 key. The Browse Mode is available on the screen.
3. Press F10 and select the Exit option from the Exit submenu.

## *Notes*

Press F10 and select the Fields submenu to Lock a number of fields on the left or the Freeze Field option to allow changes only to one field.

Press F10 and select the Go To submenu to move the cursor to the top, bottom, or record number within the file. Also, use the submenu to search the file in the specified field for a specified value.

Include the NOAPPEND clause to prevent the user from adding new records. Attempted changes cause the computer to beep.

### *Caution*

Pressing Esc or Ctrl-Q after making changes in the
Browse screen does not save the changes to the file on
disk. The datafile must be closed before you end the
dBASE IV session.

# = CALCULATE =

### *Purpose*

Performs math with all or selected records in the open
datafile. Use the Average command to get an average
for specified fields.

### *Reminder*

The datafile must include at least one numeric field.

### *Command Syntax*

**CALCULATE** [<*scope*>] <*option-list*> [FOR
<*condition*>] [WHILE <condition>] [TO <*memvar-
list*>/**TO ARRAY** <*array-name*>]

**AVERAGE** [*expN-list*] [<*scope*>] [FOR <*condition*>]
[WHILE <*condition*>] [TO <*memvar-list*>/**TO
ARRAY** <*array-name*>]

**COUNT** [TO <*memvar*>] [<*scope*>] [FOR
<*condition*>] [WHILE <*condition*>]

**SUM** [<*expN-list*>] [TO <*memvar-list*>/**TO ARRAY**
<*array-name*>] [<*scope*>] [FOR <*condition*>]
[WHILE <*condition*>]

### *Procedures*

#### *From the Dot Prompt:*

1.  Open the datafile.
2.  Display the sum of a numeric field in the open
    datafile. For example, CALCULATE (SALESAMT
    + TAXAMT) TO TOT_SALES FOR DEPT=
    201 from the dot prompt tells dBASE IV to

accumulate the total sales figures for department 201 and store the value in TOT_SALES.

3. Display the average of a numeric field. For example, the command `AVERAGE (SALESAMT + TAXAMT) TO AVG_SALE FOR DEPT = "201"` will calculate the average sales for department 201 and place the value in AVG_SALE.

4. Close the open datafile with the USE or CLOSE command before ending the dBASE IV session.

### *From the Control Center:*

1. Press the down arrow to position the bounce bar on a file. Press Enter twice to open the datafile.

2. Press the right arrow to move the bounce bar to the Create option. Press Enter to move to a query screen for the datafile. The set of boxes at the bottom identifies the fields included in the query. This is called the View. All database fields are included in the View when you begin a query.

3. Position the bounce bar in a numeric column and type `MIN`. Press F2 to query the datafile for the record with the smallest number in that field.

4. Press Esc to exit the View. When asked if you want to save the query, select the No option and return to the Control Center.

### *Note*

Remember, queries do not change the original datafile; they create a temporary file. If you desire, you can name and save this file. *<option-list>* of CALCULATE may be AVG (*<expN>*), CNT( ), MAX (*<expN>*), MIN (*expN>*), NPV (*<rate>*,*<flow>*,*<initial>*), STD (*<expN>*), SUM (*<exp>*), or VAR (*<expN>*).

# CALL

### *Purpose*

Performs special tasks by running binary programs that are written in a programming language other than dBASE IV.

*Reminder*

The program must be read from disk into memory with the LOAD command. Run the program by issuing a CALL command. Then remove it from memory with the RELEASE MODULE command.

*Command Syntax*

CALL  *<module-name>* [WITH *<variable>*]

*Procedures*

***From the Dot Prompt:***

1. Use the LOAD command to read the binary program from the disk.
2. Use the CALL command line to run the binary program.
3. When the program ends, issue the RELEASE MODULE command to remove the binary program from computer memory. If you need it again, perform the three command lines again.

***From the Control Center:***

There is no similar capability from the Control Center.

*Note*

The non-dBASE IV program must be loaded with the LOAD command before it can be run with the CALL command.

*Caution*

When it is no longer needed, always remove the loaded program from computer memory. Otherwise, you may experience an "Out of Memory" error while running an application.

# CANCEL

*Purpose*

Stops a program and closes all open programs. The dot prompt returns immediately.

## Reminder

Use the CANCEL command to stop processing the application. The user is returned to the dot prompt or Control Center.

## Command Syntax

CANCEL

## Procedures

### From the Dot Prompt:

1. Include the CANCEL command in a program to cancel the program and return control to the dot prompt or Control Center.
2. Place the CANCEL command within an IF, ENDIF or DO CASE, ENDCASE command set to allow conditional execution of the CANCEL command. Or press Esc after typing in a single command. When asked, Cancel, Suspend, or Ignore select Cancel to return to the dot prompt.

### From the Control Center:

Press the Esc key to stop processing of a query, report, or program. When asked to Cancel, Suspend, or Ignore, select Cancel to return to the Control Center.

## Notes

This command does not close databases' open files.

All private memory variables are released before control returns to the dot prompt or Control Center. To save private variables, use SUSPEND rather than CANCEL.

Use the RETURN command in programs when you want to go back to the program (or dot prompt) that initiated the program containing the RETURN command.

## Caution

Enclose each of these commands within an IF, ENDIF or DO CASE, ENDCASE command set. Otherwise, the CANCEL is encountered immediately.

# CHANGE

See **EDIT**

# CLEAR

### *Purpose*

Removes information from the screen or computer memory.

### *Reminder*

The CLEAR command causes dBASE IV to remove the specified information. For example, CLEAR MENUS removes all menus that have been defined during the dBASE IV session.

### *Command Syntax*

**CLEAR** [ALL/FIELDS/GETS/MEMORY/MENUS/ POPUPS/TYPEAHEAD/WINDOWS]

### *Procedures*

#### *From the Dot Prompt:*

1. Include the ALL clause to close open datafiles and to release all memory variables, arrays, pop-ups, and menu definitions. Issuing the CLEAR ALL command is like starting a new dBASE IV session.
2. To remove information selectively, use the appropriate clause. For example, CLEAR WINDOWS removes the window definitions from memory, as well as the screen.

#### *From the Control Center:*

There is no similar capability from the Control Center submenus.

### *Note*

Using the CLEAR command without any of the options only clears the screen. All information remains in memory.

## Caution

The CLEAR ALL command line removes everything that is currently in memory. If a memory variable that is used by a program is removed accidentally, it causes a "Variable does not exist" error.

# CLOSE

## Purpose

Closes an open datafile in a work area and saves all changes. Also closes Alternate, Format, Index and Procedure files.

## Reminders

Issue the USE or CLOSE commands to close open datafiles.

When you need to use several dBASE IV datafiles at the same time, open each one in a separate work area. dBASE IV provides 10 work areas. Identify them by letters (a through j) or numbers (1 through 10) or assign alias names (similar to file or field names).

## Command Syntax

CLOSE  ALL/ALTERNATE/DATABASES/
    FORMAT/INDEX/PROCEDURE

## Procedures

### From the Dot Prompt:

1. Open at least one datafile with the USE command.
2. Read, change, or report on information in the datafile.
3. Use CLOSE DATABASES to close all open datafiles.

### From the Control Center:

1. Position the bounce bar on a datafile name in the Data column.
2. Perform your work with the open datafile.
3. Position the bounce bar on the file and press Enter twice to close the selected datafile.

### Note

Consider closing and reopening datafiles during a data entry session so a power failure or accident does not affect your data.

### Cautions

Work area 10 is automatically assigned when you use a catalog.

Never turn off the machine until all datafiles are closed. Otherwise, you are likely to damage the datafile so you lose much of the data.

# COMPILE

### Purpose

Changes a program from readable source code to object code.

### Reminder

Before dBASE IV runs a program, it checks the date and time stamp of the .PRG (source) file to the .DBO (object) file. If they do not agree, the source program must be recompiled to utilize the most recent changes.

### Command Syntax

COMPILE  *<file-name>* [RUNTIME]

### Procedures

#### From the Dot Prompt:

Save the new or changed program on disk. When the dot prompt returns, use the COMPILE command to initiate the compiler.

#### From the Control Center:

Select Save and run the program from the Exit submenu. If the program was changed, the date and time stamp on the source file differs from the object file and dBASE IV automatically recompiles the program.

*Note*

Use the SET DEVELOPMENT command to turn on or off automatic program compilation.

*Caution*

Each command line in the program is checked for proper syntax during the compilation process. If an error is encountered, a message and the line number on which the error occurred are displayed on the screen. Errors abort the program compilation process. Change the program and try it again.

# CONTINUE

See **LOCATE**

# CONVERT

*Purpose*

Changes the structure of a single user datafile by adding a new field for multiuser access.

*Reminder*

Once the datafile is converted to be multiuser, it need not be converted again. The _dbaselock stores the following values:

| | |
|---|---|
| Count | A 2-byte hexadecimal number used to record the number of times the record is changed. |
| Time | A 3-byte hexadecimal number that records the time a lock occurred. |
| Date | A 3-byte hexadecimal number that records the date a lock occurred. |
| Name | Log-in name of the user that locked the record. |

*Command Syntax*
## CONVERT [TO <*expN*>]

*Procedures*
### From the Dot Prompt:
1. Use the CONVERT command to insert a character field called _dbaselock in the datafile structure.
2. Write a program to prompt for a customer number.
3. Use SEEK or FIND to locate the proper record. If it is found, allow record modification. dBASE IV records the count, time, date, and user in the _dbaselock field.
4. When changes are completed, issue an UNLOCK command to release the record to other users.

### From the Control Center:
There is no similar capability available through the Control Center submenus.

*Note*
> If the record is requested by more than one user, display a message to the second user regarding the lock-out condition. Then let the user choose to wait for the record or continue with other work.

*Caution*
> Locking a record before making a change prevents other people from making changes to the record at the same time. Otherwise, all changes made are not saved on disk. Only the last set of changes will be recorded.

# ═COPY

*Purpose*
> Makes a duplicate of all, or a selected set of, the datafile.

*Reminder*
> Use a COPY command or a query to create datafiles that

include only the information that you need for your
work.

## Command Syntax

COPY TO *<file-name>* [[TYPE] *<file-type>*] [FIELDS
  *<field-list>*] [*<scope>*] [FOR *<condition>*] [WHILE
  *<condition>*]

COPY STRUCTURE TO *<file-name>* [FIELDS
  *<field-list>*]

COPY TO *<file-name>* STRUCTURE EXTENDED

COPY TO ARRAY *<array-name>* [FIELDS *<field-
  list>*] [*<scope>*] [FOR *<condition>*] [WHILE
  *<condition>*]

COPY FILE *<file-name>* TO *<file-name>*

COPY INDEXES *<index-file-list>* [TO *<multiple-
  index>*]

COPY MEMO *<memo-field-name>* TO *<file-name>*
  [ADDITIVE]

COPY TAG *<tag-name>* [OF *<multiple-file-name>*]
  TO *<index-file-name>*

## Procedures

### From the Dot Prompt:
1. Open one of the datafiles with the USE command.
2. Issue the COPY TO command to create a file from
   the open one.
3. Close the open datafile.

### From the Control Center:
1. Open the datafile.
2. Use a query to create a new datafile of selected
   records.
3. Use the Catalog submenu to create a duplicate of a
   file.

*Notes*

An array must be established with the DECLARE
command. Then use the COPY TO ARRAY command
to hold data from at least one record from the open
datafile. Refer to each item by its subscript.

# COUNT

See **CALCULATE**

# CREATE APPLICATION

*Purpose*

Designs and uses the dBASE IV Applications Generator
to write programs.

*Reminder*

Applications created through the Applications Generator
may need modifications. Use the MODIFY command to
change a program.

*Command Syntax*

**CREATE/MODIFY APPLICATION** *<file-name>*/?

*Procedures*

**From the Dot Prompt:**

1. Issue CREATE APPLICATION to access the
   Applications Generator.
2. A window opens and input areas are available for
   the Application name, Description, Main menu type
   and name, Database/View, and Index/Order
   information. If you use multiple index files, you
   must specify the main index in the ORDER input
   area.

3. When all input areas are correct, press Ctrl-End.
4. Supply information for the sign-on screen.
5. Open the menu and select Application/Generate Quick Application.
6. A window opens. Fill in the data, screen format, report format, label format, index files, and main menu names. Press Ctrl-End when all input areas are correct. Press a key when prompted.
7. Select Yes to generate the application.
8. Position the bounce bar on the Save Current Application Definition option to save the application on disk.
9. Exit from the Applications Generator.
10. Issue a DO command to see the results of your work.

***From the Control Center:***

1. Select the Create option in the Applications column. When prompted, press A to select the Applications Generator.
2. Create the application by following the dot prompt procedure, steps 2 through 9.
3. Run the application by selecting the option from the Applications column of the Control Center screen.

___
***Note***

Use the Applications Generator to create quickly an application for the user to maintain and report information kept in the datafile.

# CREATE FROM

___
***Purpose***

Creates a new dBASE IV datafile from another datafile.

___
***Reminder***

Consider using the COPY STRUCTURE command to create a duplicate of the current database structure.

### Command Syntax
CREATE *<file-name>* FROM *<extended-structure-file>*

### Procedures
#### From the Dot Prompt:
1. Use the CREATE FROM command to specify the name of the datafile to be created from the datafile that contains the field information.
2. When the dot prompt returns, the new datafile is available on the disk.

#### From the Control Center:
There is no equivalent capability from the submenus.

### Notes
Issue the COPY STRUCTURE command from the dot prompt to create an empty datafile structure from another datafile.

Use a query to create an empty datafile structure from another datafile. It is the only way to create a new structure.

### Caution
Each field must be described by a record in the extended structure datafile. Otherwise, the new datafile is not created properly.

# CREATE/MODIFY LABEL

### Purpose
Designs and prints labels for an open datafile.

### Reminder
If the specified label form file exists on the disk, the MODIFY LABEL command lets you change it. If the specified form file exists on the disk, the CREATE LABEL command will ask if you want to modify it.

---

## *Command Syntax*
### CREATE/MODIFY LABEL
   *<file-name>*/?

---

## *Procedures*
### *From the Dot Prompt:*
1. Issue the CREATE LABEL command to design a new screen format.
2. Press F10 to access the menu line at the top of the screen.
3. From the Dimensions submenu, select Predefined Size and a label type. Press Enter.
4. Open the Fields submenu and select Add Field to select field names.
5. Select the fields for your labels. When asked for template information, press Ctrl-End.
6. Open the Layout submenu and select Save This Label Design option.
7. When prompted, supply a name for the label format.
8. Open the Print submenu and select Begin Printing.
9. Now open the Exit submenu and select the Save Changes and Exit option to return to the dot prompt.

### *From the Control Center:*
1. Open a datafile by pressing Enter twice in the data column.
2. Select the Create option in the Labels column.
3. Follow the dot prompt example (steps 2 through 9) to create and save the label format.

---

## *Notes*
Use the MODIFY LABEL command to change an existing label file. Position the record pointer or search with the Go To submenu.

Use the print submenu to control printing options.

Adjust the distance between labels by selecting the Spaces Between Label Columns option from the Dimensions submenu.

# CREATE/MODIFY QUERY/VIEW

## *Purpose*

Extracts records from datafiles for use. Sometimes, you
need the same information every month. For example,
you may need to review the names of customers who are
ready to renew subscriptions or budget data.

## *Reminder*

If the specified query file does not exist on the disk, the
MODIFY QUERY command lets you create it.

## *Command Syntax*

**CREATE/MODIFY  QUERY** *<file-name>*/?

**CREATE/MODIFY  VIEW** *<file-name>*/?

## *Procedures*

### *From the Dot Prompt:*

1. Include the ? clause to open a window of existing
   query files.
2. Select a query from the list.

### *From the Control Center:*

1. Open a datafile. Press the right arrow to select the
   Create option in the queries column.
2. Press F10 and select Add File to Query. Select a
   second datafile. Move the highlighted input area to
   the key field in a datafile.
3. Select the Create Link by Pointing option.
4. Press F3 (up) F4 (down) to move to the other file
   layout. Place the input area where LINK1 is
   displayed in the field column.
5. Use the F5 key to add fields from the new datafile
   to the view.
6. Complete the query definition, press F10, and select
   Save This Query. Type the query name in the
   input area.
7. Press F2 to begin the search of the data.

## *Notes*

Do not exceed 20 calculations per query screen.

If necessary, provide several lines of conditions for one or more fields. Press the down arrow to move to the next line.

Select the Sort on This Field option from the Fields submenu to provide a sorted set of datafile records.

# CREATE/MODIFY REPORT

### Purpose
Designs and uses report forms to print records from the open datafile(s). Prints columnar reports, special forms, and Mailmerge documents.

### Reminders
Sketch a report, form, or label that you need to print from the data in the datafile.

If the specified Report file does not exist on the disk, the MODIFY REPORT command lets you create it. If the specified Report file does exist on the disk, CREATE REPORT lets you modify it.

### Command Syntax
CREATE/MODIFY REPORT *<file-name>*/?

### Procedures
#### From the Dot Prompt:
1. Issue the CREATE REPORT command to design a new datafile screen format.
2. Press F10, select the layout, and select the Quick Layouts option.
3. Select Column Layout. A columnar report format with all fields in the datafile appears. The field name is the column heading.
4. Press F10 and use the menus to customize your report. When satisfied, select Layout/Save This Report, supply a name, and press Enter.

5. Use the MODIFY REPORT command to change an existing screen file format.
6. When a report form exists, use the REPORT FORM command to send the report to the screen. Add the TO PRINT option to send the report to a printer.

*From the Control Center:*
1. Open the datafile. Select the Create option in the Reports column.
2. Select Quick Layouts from the Layout menu.
3. Follow the dot prompt procedures to change the form, as in steps 3 and 4.
4. From the Control Center screen, select the file name from the Reports column.
5. When asked, select Print Report. The report is sent to the printer.

---

*Notes*

The Page Header Band identifies the information that must print at the top of each page.

If you want the report to begin with a cover letter, title page, or some other document, use the Report Intro Band. The information is printed one time at the beginning of the report.

Use the Detail Band to specify the fields to be printed on the report. The layout is used each time a record is printed from the open datafile.

The Report Summary Band identifies totals, counts, etc., that must be printed at the end of the report. Include labels for the summary information too. For example, print `Total Sales` next to the summary field.

Use the Page Footer Band to specify information that you want printed at the bottom of each page.

Print information from several datafiles by specifying the fields from the first datafile. Then select the Use Different Database File or View option from the Layout submenu. The new datafile name is displayed on the status line as the open datafile. Any new fields you put on the report form are from the open datafile.

Select the Form Layout option when you need to provide one record per page. For example, use it to print a bill or purchase order.

Use the Box option from the Layout submenu to print a box on the report page.

Use the Band submenu to specify at least one field to group the information on the report.

Change the print style or position, insert a line, remove a line, add a line, or insert a page break by selecting options from the Words submenu.

Move the record pointer or search a field for a specific value by selecting options from the Go To submenu.

Access the printer through the Print submenu. Begin Printing, Eject Page Now, and Use Print Form { } are a few of the options available.

### Cautions

Do not put column headings within the Detail Band. Anything within this band is printed for each record.

If you are using 8 1/2-by-11-inch paper and your report is wider than 132 columns, columns must be removed from the layout. An 8 1/2-by-11-inch sheet of paper accommodates 80 positions in the normal print font or 132 positions in condensed print. An 11-by-14-inch sheet of paper accommodates 132 positions in normal print or 210 positions in condensed print.

# CREATE/MODIFY SCREEN

### Purpose

Designs and saves record maintenance screens that include meaningful labels. Used rather than the Browse screen.

## Reminders

Sketch your screen layout for the datafile before you begin.

If the specified screen file does not exist on the disk, the MODIFY SCREEN command lets you create it.   If the specified screen file exists on the disk, the CREATE SCREEN command asks whether you want to modify the file.

## Command Syntax

CREATE/MODIFY  SCREEN <file-name>/?

## Procedures

### From the Dot Prompt:

1.  Type USE and the name of the database for which you want to design a screen format.
2.  Use CREATE or MODIFY SCREEN to design or change a datafile screen format.
3.  Press F10 to access the menu line at the top of the screen.
4.  Select Quick Layout to create a new screen format.
5.  Use the submenus to change the screen format.
6.  Save the screen format by selecting Save Changes and Exit.

### From the Control Center:

1.  Open the datafile.
2.  Select Create from the Forms column.
3.  Create and save the screen format for the open datafile, as shown in Dot Prompt Procedures steps 3 through 5.
4.  From the Control Center, select the file name from the Forms column.

## Notes

Select Fields/Modify Field/<field-name-to-modify>/ Template to restrict data entry characteristics (numbers only, uppercase, etc.).

Select Fields/Modify Field/*<field-name to modify>*/
Picture to restrict information. For example, restrict the
STATE field to accept only proper state names.

Select the Fields/Modify Field/*<field-name-to-modify>*/
Edit options to provide default values or deny edit
privileges.

To move an area on the screen format, use the F6,
arrow, and Enter keys to specify the entire area and its
contents. Then use the F7, arrow, and Enter keys to
move the selected area to another part of the screen.

### Caution

Unless you specify that you want to use the screen
format, the Browse or Append screens are used. From
the Control Center, open the datafile, and then select the
form. From the dot prompt, open the datafile and then
use the SET FORMAT command with the format name.

# CREATE/MODIFY STRUCTURE

### Purpose

Creates or changes a layout for a dBASE IV datafile.

### Reminders

Identify the information that you want to keep in a
dBASE IV datafile. This task is easier if you lay out
your reports first.

Assign meaningful names to each data item. The name
must begin with a letter, be no longer than 11 characters,
and contain only letters, numbers, and/or underscore
symbols.

Decide on field types (Character, Date, Logical, Memo,
Numeric, Float).

Finally, decide the largest possible number of characters
you expect the field to need.

*Command Syntax*

CREATE *<file-name>*

MODIFY STRUCTURE

*Procedures*

*From the Dot Prompt:*

1. Type CREATE and a file name to create a new datafile. A blank structure is displayed for your field information.
2. Type the name, type, and length for each field to be kept in the datafile. Press Ctrl-W to return to the dot prompt and keep the new structure.
3. Change the datafile structure at any time. First, open the datafile with the USE command. Then issue the MODIFY STRUCTURE command.

*From the Control Center:*

1. Select the Create option in the Data column. A datafile structure input form is presented on the screen.
2. Type the information for each field in the input areas.
3. Press Ctrl-N to insert a new field or Ctrl-U to delete a field.
4. Press Enter or Ctrl-W to return to the Control Center. When prompted, type a file name for your new file.
5. When asked whether you want to input data, press N or Y.

*Note*

Add new fields, delete fields, and change the field lengths as your needs change.

*Caution*

Do not change a field name that contains data currently. dBASE IV matches the old structure to the new structure by field name. If the names do not match, the data from the old file is not copied to the new file.

# DEACTIVATE MENU

See **DEFINE MENU**

# DEACTIVATE POPUP

See **DEFINE POPUP**

# DEACTIVATE WINDOW

See **DEFINE WINDOW**

# DEBUG

## *Purpose*

Tests new or changed dBASE IV programs.

## *Reminders*

When you write a new program or make a change to an existing program, it may not run the first time. Each command in the program must follow proper syntax.

Use dBASE IV's fullscreen debugger to debug programs. Its windows allow you to run a program and watch it run.

## *Command Syntax*

**DEBUG** *<file-name>/<procedure-name>* [WITH *<parameter-list>*]

## *Procedures*

### *From the Dot Prompt:*

1.  Use the DEBUG command to run the program or procedure.

2.  The box in the upper left corner displays the program. The highlighted bar identifies the next command to be performed.
3.  The box at the top right is the command box. Use it as a reference to specify the next action.
4.  Use the DISPLAY box to specify fields, variables, and arrays as they are affected while you step through the program.
5.  The DEBUGGER window displays information about the datafile, procedure, and program as you step through the program.

***From the Control Center:***

These commands are for programs only. Equivalent capabilities do not exist from the Control Center.

*Note*

Include the SUSPEND command in a program to stop the program temporarily. The dot prompt is available for you to display or change memory variables, datafile records, or any combination of information. Use RESUME to continue running your program.

*Caution*

Remove all debugging commands before making it available to the users.

# DECLARE

*Purpose*

Establishes an array. This command specifies the name, length, and width of the array. For example, SALESRECS[10,3] creates an array called SALESRECS that is 10 lines long and 3 fields wide.

*Reminders*

An array is like a table that is kept in memory.

Use subscripts to address the array elements. For example, SALESRECS[3,2] specifies the third row and second column of the array elements.

### Command Syntax

DECLARE *<array-name-1>* [{*<number-of- rows,*}
{*<number-of-columns>*}] {*<array-name-2>*
[{*<number-of-rows>,*} { *<number-of-columns>*}] ...}

### Procedures

#### From the Dot Prompt:

1. Issue the DECLARE command from the dot prompt or in a program to create an array.
2. Set the value of the elements with the = or STORE command.

#### From the Control Center:

There is no equivalent capability from the Control Center submenus.

### Note

Use the DISPLAY MEMORY or ? command to see the values in the array.

# DEFINE BAR

See **DEFINE POPUP**

# DEFINE BOX

### Purpose

Defines a box that can be printed on the printer to enhance the appearance of a report.

### Reminder

dBASE IV provides border choices of a single or double line.

*Command Syntax*

**DEFINE BOX FROM** <*print-column*> **TO** <*print-column*> **HEIGHT** <*expN*> [AT LINE <*print-line*>] [SINGLE/DOUBLE/<*border-definition-string*>]

*Procedures*

*From the dot prompt:*

1. Issue the DEFINE BOX command from the dot prompt or in a program. Specify the line number, column number, and character to be used for the border.
2. dBASE IV provides SINGLE and DOUBLE line options, but you also can specify any printable character for the border.
3. Set the _box memory variable to True when you want to print the box. When the print advances past the lines specified in the DEFINE BOX command, the box is printed on the page.

*From the Control Center:*

Select the Box option from the Layout submenu when creating a report format.

*Caution*

Do not specify a box too large for the paper. dBASE IV continues it on the next page.

# DEFINE MENU, DEFINE PAD

*Purpose*

A set of commands used to build bounce bar menus.

*Reminders*

Use bounce bar menus to reduce user typing and improve data validation.

Combine the DEFINE MENU, DEFINE PAD, and ACTIVATE MENU commands to create the menu.

## Command Syntax

**DEFINE MENU** <*menu-name*> [MESSAGE <*expC*>]

**DEFINE PAD** <*pad-name*> **OF** <*menu-name*>
**PROMPT** <*expC*> [AT <*row*>,<*col*>] [MESSAGE
<*expC*>]

**ACTIVATE MENU** <*menu-name*> [**PAD**<*pad-
name*>]

**DEACTIVATE MENU**

**ON SELECTION PAD**<*pad-name*> **OF** <*menu-
name*> [<*command*>]

**SHOW MENU**<*menu-name*> [PAD <*pad-name*>]

## Procedures

### From the Dot Prompt:

1.  Use **DEFINE MENU** to begin the menu command
    set and assign it a name.
2.  Each **DEFINE PAD** command line identifies a
    menu option. It also provides an option name,
    prompt, and screen positioning. For example, the
    following command lines define a vertical menu
    called MENU1:

```
DEFINE MENU MENU1
DEFINE PAD MAINT OF MENU1 PROMPT
   "File Maintenance" AT 5,22
DEFINE PAD REPORTS OF MENU1
   PROMPT "Report Menu" AT 7,22
DEFINE PAD UTILITY OF MENU1
   PROMPT "Utilities Menu" AT
   9,22
DEFINE PAD ENDIT OF MENU1 PROMPT
   "Exit Application" AT 11,223
```

3.  Each **DEFINE PAD** command should have an **ON
    SELECTION PAD** command as shown:

```
ON SELECTION PAD MAINT of MENU1
   DO MAINT
```

```
ON SELECTION PAD REPORTS OF MENU1
   DO PRTRPTS
   . .
   .
   .
```

4.  Activate the menu as follows:

```
ACTIVATE MENU MENU1
```

5.  When finished with a menu, use the DEACTIVATE
    MENU command.

***From the Control Center:***

When you create an application through the Application
column of the Control Center, you are given the choice
of using a vertical (bar) or horizontal (pop-up) menu.

───────────
*Notes*

Use the ACTIVATE MENU command to provide a
menu to the user. The DEACTIVATE MENU command
erases the menu from the screen but not memory.

The SHOW MENU command displays the specified
menu on the screen. However, the menu is not available
to the user.

Include an ON SELECTION PAD command for each
menu option to identify the action to be taken when the
user selects the option.  When the menu is active, use the
right- and left-arrow keys to select each menu item.
Press Enter to activate the selected menu item.

───────────
*Caution*

Include the RELEASE MENU command in the program
to remove the menu definition from memory. Otherwise,
you may experience an "Out of Memory" error while
running an application.

# DEFINE POPUP

## Purpose

Provides a window that contains specific information, messages, and a border.

## Reminder

Combine the DEFINE POPUP, DEFINE BAR, and ACTIVATE POPUP commands to create the submenu.

## Command Syntax

**DEFINE POPUP** <popup-name> **FROM** <row-1>,<col-1> [**TO** <row-2>,<col-2>] [PROMPT FIELD <field-name>/PROMPT FILES [LIKE <skeleton>]/PROMPT STRUCTURE] [MESSAGE <expC>]

**ACTIVATE POPUP** <popup-name>

**DEACTIVATE POPUP**

**DEFINE BAR** <line-number> **OF** <popup-name> **PROMPT** <expC>[MESSAGE <expC>] [SKIP [FOR <condition>]]

**ON SELECTION POPUP** <popup-name>/**ALL** [<command>]

**SHOW POPUP** <popup-name>

## Procedures

### From the Dot Prompt:

1. Use DEFINE POPUP to begin a pop-up definition.
2. Include PROMPT FIELD to identify the field values for a datafile.
3. Include PROMPT FILES to open a window with a directory listing.
4. Each DEFINE BAR command line identifies a submenu option. The line number, pop-up name, and user prompt are also included.

### From the Control Center:

When you create an application through the Application column of the Control Center, choose between a horizontal (pop-up) or vertical (bar) menu.

### Notes

Use the ACTIVATE POPUP command to provide a pop-up to the user. The DEACTIVATE POPUP command erases the pop-up from the screen but not memory.

The SHOW POPUP command displays the specified pop-up menu on the screen. However, the menu is not available to the user.

Include an ON SELECTION POPUP command for each option to identify the action to be taken when the user selects the option.

Use bounce bar submenus as often as possible to prevent the user from having to type. Checking for a valid user response is unnecessary.

### Caution

Include the RELEASE POPUP command in the program to remove the pop-up definition from memory. Otherwise, you may experience an "Out of Memory" error while running an application.

# DEFINE WINDOW

### Purpose

Provides a defined area of information on the screen for the user. Allows you to define borders and colors of screen windows.

### Reminder

Define and use windows to restrict the user's attention (and response) to a selected area of information.

## *Command Syntax*

DEFINE WINDOW <window-name> FROM
<row-1>,<col-1> TO <row-2>,<col-2>[DOUBLE/
PANEL/NONE/<border-definition-string>] [COLOR
[<standard>] [,<enhanced>] [,<frame>]]

ACTIVATE WINDOW <window-name-list>/ALL

DEACTIVATE WINDOW <window-name-list>/ALL

MOVE WINDOW <window-name> TO <row>,
<column>/BY <delta-row>,<delta-column>

## *Procedures*

### *From the Dot Prompt:*

1. Use the DEFINE WINDOW command to draw a
   box on the screen. Specify a name, area, type, and
   colors for the box.
2. Provide the name of the defined window in the
   ACTIVATE WINDOW command line when you
   want to display it on the screen.
3. Issue the MOVE WINDOW command to move the
   window absolutely (TO) or relatively (BY).
4. Issue a DEACTIVATE WINDOW command to
   remove the window from the screen. The
   information that was overlaid returns to the screen
   for the user.

### *From the Control Center:*

When you create an application through the Application
column of the Control Center, you may define a window
as in DOT PROMPT.

## *Note*

Use the MOVE WINDOW command to reposition it on
the screen.

## *Caution*

Include the RELEASE WINDOW command in the
program to remove window definitions from memory.
Otherwise, you may experience an "Out of Memory"
error while running an application.

# DELETE

## *Purpose*

Flags records for removal from the open datafile.

## *Reminder*

Marking records for deletion does not remove them from the datafile. If you want to remove all marked records from the file, type PACK from the dot prompt and press Enter.

## *Command Syntax*

**DELETE** [*<scope>*] [FOR *<condition>*] [WHILE *<condition>*]

**PACK**

## *Procedures*

### *From the Dot Prompt:*

1.  Open a datafile. Use the GO command to move to the record you want removed from the datafile.
2.  Display the record to see that it is the correct record.
3.  Type DELETE and press Enter.
4.  Display the record again. Notice the asterisk (*) between the record number and the first field value. The asterisk marks or identifies this record for removal from the datafile.
5.  Type PACK and press Enter to actually remove the marked record.

### *From the Control Center:*

1.  Open a datafile and press F2 to use the Browse screen.
2.  Use the arrow keys to move to the record to be removed from the datafile.
3.  Press F10, then press the down arrow to position the bounce bar to Mark Record for Deletion, and press Enter. Notice that Del appears on the right section of the status line.

4. Press F10 again. Use Clear Deletion Mark to remove the deletion flag.
5. Select the Exit option from the Exit submenu to return to the Control Center.

*Notes*

Because the PACK operation takes a little time, mark several records for deletion before issuing the PACK command.

Limit the effect of the DELETE and RECALL commands by specifying a condition. For example, DELETE ALL FOR STATE = "CA" from the dot prompt marks for deletion all records that contain "CA" in the state field.

# DELETE FILE

See **ERASE**

# DELETE TAG

*Purpose*

Removes a tag from a multiple index file.

*Reminder*

A multiple index file contains a maximum of 47 tags (sort orders).

*Command Syntax*

**DELETE TAG** *<tag-name-1>* [OF *<multiple-index-file-name>*]/*<index-file-name-1>* [,*<tag-name-2>* [OF *<multiple-index-file-name>*]/*<index-file-name-2>* ...]

### Procedures

#### From the Dot Prompt:

Issue a DELETE TAG command to remove a tag name from a multiple index file.

#### From the Control Center:

From the Modify Structure screen, select the Remove Unwanted Index Tag option from the Organize submenu to remove tags from the multiple index file.

### Note

Include multiple tag names in a DELETE TAG command.

### Caution

Specify a proper tag name in the DELETE TAG command line. Otherwise, dBASE IV reports an error.

# =DIR

### Purpose

Performs a directory operation that is available from the Dot prompt. For example, lists the datafiles on the disk without ending the dBASE IV session.

### Reminder

Although dBASE IV provides several dot prompt commands and Control Center submenu options, you are not limited to those capabilities. Run any DOS command from the dot prompt with the RUN or ! command. From the Control Center, select the Tools/ DOS Utilities/DOS Menu Selections to perform any DOS commands.

### Command Syntax

**DIRECTORY/DIR** [[ON] *<drive>*:] [[LIKE] [*<path>*] *<skeleton>*]

### *Procedures*

#### *From the Dot Prompt:*

Use the DIR command to list files on the current disk.
For example, DIR C:*.COM lists all files on drive C
with a .COM extension. Issue the DIR command
without any of the options to list only the datafiles
(.DBF).

#### *From the Control Center:*

1. Press F10 to access the menu line at the top of the
   screen.
2. Select the Tools/DOS Utilities options. A window
   that contains file names, lengths, date, time,
   attributes, and space used appears on your screen.
   Press F10 to use the submenu options included on
   the screen.
3. Use the Files submenu to change the drive or
   subdirectory or to specify the type of files to be
   displayed in the Control Center's DOS directory
   window.

### *Note*

A DIR command without a skeleton lists only the .DBF
files on the disk.

# DISPLAY

See LIST

# DO

### *Purpose*

Runs dBASE IV programs.

### *Reminder*

Write custom programs to be used with the programs
produced with the Applications Generator. For example,

change the input screen or validate the value typed into a field on the screen before saving it on disk.

### Command Syntax

**DO** *<program-name>/<procedure-name>*
[WITH *<parameter-list>*]

### Procedures

#### From the Dot Prompt:

Run the program by issuing the DO command. If the program has changed since the last compilation, dBASE IV evaluates it for errors.

#### From the Control Center:

1. Position the bounce bar on the selected option in the Application column and press Enter.
2. When prompted, select Run Application.

### Notes

Use the Applications Generator to write programs quickly. Then modify these programs when changes are needed to make the system easier to use.

When you are finished with them in your program, remember to close your datafiles to avoid problems with your data.

### Caution

If you try to create a program with a name that already exists on disk, dBASE IV tells you that the name exists. It asks whether you want to overwrite the existing one with the current one or cancel the save operation.

# DO CASE, ENDCASE

### Purpose

Controls program flow based on data values. For example, if the record is a debit, it prints the amount in column A. Otherwise, it prints the amount in column B.

*Reminder*

The effect of this command set is the same as the IF, ENDIF command set.

*Command Syntax*

DO CASE
  CASE <condition-1>
    <commands-1>
  [CASE <condition-2>
    <commands-2>]
  [OTHERWISE <commands-3>]
ENDCASE

*Procedures*

**From the Dot Prompt:**

1. Use the DO CASE, ENDCASE command set to mark the beginning and end of a conditional situation. Each CASE command within the set is evaluated until a condition is met, or all conditions are false.

2. When one of the CASE conditions is evaluated as true, the command lines that follow it are processed and all other CASE lines are skipped. If no cases are found true, the commands after OTHERWISE are processed. Processing continues with the lines that follow the ENDCASE command.

**From the Control Center:**

Follow the steps from the Dot Prompt when generating applications.

*Note*

Include the OTHERWISE clause in the DO CASE, ENDCASE command set when you want to supply command lines for a situation that does not meet any of the CASE conditions.

# DO WHILE, ENDDO

## *Purpose*

Performs a set of command lines until some condition is met. For example, it prints a report of all records in a datafile by writing a program with several @...SAY commands.

## *Reminder*

The effect of this command set is the same as the SCAN, ENDSCAN command set. However, when processing a datafile, include the SKIP command to move the record pointer. Record pointer movement is not handled automatically.

## *Command Syntax*

DO WHILE <condition>
   <commands>
   [LOOP]
   [EXIT]
ENDDO

## *Procedures*

### *From the Dot Prompt:*

Use DO WHILE <condition> and ENDDO to establish a set of command lines you want to perform until some condition is met.

### *From the Control Center:*

Looping is done automatically when you use selections from the Queries, Forms, Reports, and Labels columns of the Control Center.

## *Notes*

Include the LOOP command within the loop in the program to force dBASE IV to reevaluate a condition. When the LOOP command is encountered, the command lines following the loop are ignored and the condition is reviewed. If the condition is still true, the loop continues.

Use EXIT to end the looping activity immediately. When this command is encountered, the program continues running with the command following the ENDDO line.

## Caution

Beware of endless loops. If the condition specified by the DO WHILE or SCAN command is never met, the loop will continue forever. If the program runs longer than you anticipate, verify that all loop conditions will end eventually.

# EDIT

## Purpose

Changes the information in an existing datafile.

## Reminders

The effect of the EDIT is the same as the CHANGE commands.

Use the following keys while editing data:

| | |
|---|---|
| Ctrl-U | Flag or unflag a record for deletion |
| Ctrl-Q | End the edit session without saving the data changes |
| Ctrl-W | End the edit session and save the data changes |
| PgUp | Move to a previous screen |
| PgDn | Move to the next screen |
| ↑ | Move to the previous field or record |
| ↓ | Move to the next field or record |
| → | Move to the next character |
| ← | Move to the previous character |
| Ctrl- ← | Move to the next field |
| Ctrl- → | Move to the previous field |

## Command Syntax

**EDIT** [NOINIT] [NOFOLLOW] [NOAPPEND]
[NOMENU] [NOEDIT] [NODELETE] [NOCLEAR]
[*<record-number>*] [FIELDS *<field-list>*] [*<scope>*]
[FOR *<condition>*] [WHILE *<condition>*]

**CHANGE** [NOINIT] [NOFOLLOW] [NOAPPEND]
[NOMENU] [NOEDIT] [NODELETE] [NOCLEAR]
[*<record-number>*] [FIELDS *<field-list>*] [*<scope>*]
[FOR *<condition>*] [WHILE *<condition>*]

## Procedures

### From the Dot Prompt:

1. Open the datafile. Use GOTO, LOCATE, FIND, or SEEK to move the record pointer to the desired record.
2. Type EDIT and press Enter to change each field of the record.
3. Change the information. Then press Ctrl-W to save the changes and return to the dot prompt.

### From the Control Center:

1. Position the bounce bar on the datafile name.
2. Press the F2 key. Use the Browse screen to edit the data.

## Notes

Include the NOINIT, NOFOLLOW, NOAPPEND, NOMENU, NOEDIT, NODELETE, and NOCLEAR clauses to control the edit activity.

Replace *<record-number>* with a valid record number. Include the FIELDS *<field-list>* clause to specify the fields to be presented on the screen. The *<scope>*, FOR *<condition>*, and WHILE *<condition>* clauses specify a range of datafile records.

## Caution

Pressing Esc or Ctrl-Q after making changes does not save the changes to the file on disk. The datafile must be closed before you end the dBASE IV session.

# EJECT, EJECT PAGE

## *Purpose*

Moves the paper in the printer to the top of the next page.

## *Reminder*

Turn on the printer because this command affects the printer, not the screen.

## *Command Syntax*

EJECT

EJECT PAGE

## *Procedures*

### *From the Dot Prompt:*

1. Issue an EJECT command. The paper moves to the top of the next page.
2. When the EJECT PAGE command is encountered, the headings and footers specified by the ON PAGE command line are printed as the printer advances to the next page.

### *From the Control Center:*

1. When you select a report from the Reports or Labels column, you are asked whether you want to print the information. Answer Yes.
2. A window of print options opens on the screen. Select the Eject Page Now option before or after selecting the Begin Printing option.

## *Note*

Use the SET DEVICE TO or SET PRINT commands to turn the printer on and off for @..SAY, ?, or ?? commands.

## *Caution*

Before you turn on your printer, adjust the paper to the top of the page. Otherwise, the paper just moves to that same line of the next page.

# ERASE

## *Purpose*

Removes a file from the disk without ending the dBASE IV session.

## *Reminder*

Because ERASE does not allow the use of wild cards with a file name, issue the DOS DEL command with wild cards from the dot prompt with the RUN or ! command.

## *Command Syntax*

ERASE  <file-name>/?

DELETE  FILE  <file-name>/?

## *Procedures*

### *From the Dot Prompt:*

Issue a DELETE FILE or ERASE command from the prompt or within a program to remove the specified file from the disk.

### *From the Control Center:*

1. Press F10 to access the menu line at the top of the screen.
2. Move the selection bar to the file(s) you desire to delete. Press Enter to mark each file.
3. Select the Tools/DOS Utilities options. A window that contains file names, file size, date, time, attributes, and space used appears on your screen. Press F10 so the DOS utilities menu line and a window of submenu options are included on the screen.
4. Open the Mark submenu to flag or unflag files. Then use the Operations submenu to delete the marked file(s).
5. Use the Exit submenu to return to the Control Center screen.

*Note*

The DELETE FILE and ERASE commands perform the
same function.

*Caution*

Always include the file extension for the file name.
Otherwise, dBASE IV displays an error message.

# EXPORT

*Purpose*

Sends dBASE IV data to other popular software
packages.

*Reminder*

Export dBASE IV data to RapidFile, dBASE II,
Framework II, or PFS: FILE.

*Command Syntax*

**EXPORT TO** *<file-name>* [TYPE] **PFS/DBASEII/**
**FW2/RPD** [FIELDS *<field-list>*] [*<scope>*] [FOR
*<condition>*] [WHILE *<condition>*]

*Procedures*

**From the Dot Prompt:**

1. Open the dBASE IV datafile that contains the data
to export.
2. At the next dot prompt, type EXPORT TO
C:\FW\SALES.FW2 TYPE FW2 to export a
dBASE IV file to a Framework II file in the FW
subdirectory on drive C.
3. Type USE to close the datafile.

**From the Control Center:**

1. Open the datafile to be used to create the new file.
2. Press the F10 key, open the Tools submenu, and
select the Export option. A window of file types is
displayed on the screen.

3. Use the arrow key to position the bounce bar on the type of file being created from the dBASE IV datafile. Press Enter to select it.
4. Type the name of the file and press Enter to start the transfer.

*Note*

If the file type that you need to use is not included in the list of the Export submenu, specify the delimiter and then select the Text Fixed-length Fields option. Most software packages can import this type of a text file.

The ASSIST Export offers Export to more file types than does the dot prompt EXPORT command.

*Caution*

The dBASE IV file structure must be created so the datafile fields are in the same order as the file receiving the data. Otherwise, you may find that your data is in the wrong fields.

═ **FIND** ═══════════════════════

*Purpose*

Looks through the data in the open file for specific information that matches the key fields used to index it.

*Reminders*

Open the datafile with an appropriate index file.

From the dot prompt, provide the search value for a FIND command in a character memory variable. Always add an ampersand symbol (&) to the front of the memory variable when using it in the FIND command line. This procedure is called macro substitution.

*Command Syntax*
    FIND  *<literal-key>*

## *Procedures*

### *From the Dot Prompt:*

1.  Open the datafile with its index file. For example,
    type `USE SUBSCRPT INDEX SUBSCRPT` and
    press Enter.
2.  Store the search value in a memory variable
    preceded by an ampersand. For example, the
    following command lines create a character
    memory variable and use it to locate the value in
    the datafile:

    ```
    STORE NAME TO MKEY
    FIND &MKEY
    IF FOUND( )
    ```

3.  If the record found is not the one you want, type
    `SKIP` and press Enter to move to the next record in
    the datafile. Then display that record.
4.  Close the open datafile by typing `USE` and pressing
    Enter.

### *From the Control Center:*

1.  Highlight the datafile to use, press Enter, and
    choose Display Data. Press Enter to move the
    bounce bar to the field you want to search.
2.  Press F10 to access the menu at the top of the
    screen. Open the Go To submenu and select the
    Forward Search option.
3.  When asked for the search string, type it in the
    input area and press Enter. If it is not found, the
    computer beeps and tells you that the value was not
    found in the datafile.
4.  Press Esc to return to the Go To submenu.
    Otherwise, the submenus are removed and the
    bounce bar is positioned on the requested record.
5.  Return to the Control Center by pressing the Esc
    key or selecting the Exit option from the Exit
    submenu.

## *Notes*

Uppercase and lowercase letters must be considered
when you are providing search criteria. If the Control

Center's Match Capitalization option in the Settings submenu equals Yes, or the dot prompt's SET EXACT command is turned ON, all character positions must match in case as well as length.

If you prefer to search the datafile for a value, or its nearest value, use the SET NEAR ON environment command. If the specified value does not exist, dBASE IV returns the nearest match rather than an end-of-file condition.

From the dot prompt, you may FIND a part of the field. For example, if you want to find Smith, you may store S to a memory variable and issue the FIND command. You will find the first last name beginning with S.

### *Caution*

When using a search command in a program, use the EOF( ) or FOUND( ) functions in an IF command to determine whether the desired record was found during the search. Otherwise, you may be processing the wrong record.

# FUNCTION

### *Purpose*

A section of a program that performs specialized tasks.

### *Reminders*

A function is a set of commands that are performed at least twice from a program so repeating a set of commands is unnecessary.

dBASE IV provides a set of functions that performs specialized tasks. For example, the EOF( ) function tests whether you have encountered the end of file.

### *Command Syntax*

FUNCTION  *<procedure-name>*

## Procedures

### From the Dot Prompt:

A function is identified by the FUNCTION command as the first line and the RETURN( ) command as the last line. The RETURN( ) command line must send information back to the calling program or procedure.

For example, the Headers procedure in the following command lines uses a function called Centered. The procedure sends the width of the page and the value to be centered on that page. The function includes the PARAMETERS command to accept the information from the calling procedure.

```
procedure headers
   lncnt = 5
   @ lncnt,01 say date( )
   mtemp = "ABC MAIL-OUT COMPANY"
   @ lncnt,centered(80,mtemp) say
   mtemp
   return

function centered( )
   parameters mcols, mvalue
   mnum = ((mcols-len(mvalue))/2)
   return(mnum)
```

The CENTERED( ) user-defined function calculates and returns the column needed to center the value across the page.

### From the Control Center:

There is no equivalent capability from the Control Center.

## Notes

Identify a user-defined function by including the FUNCTION command line at the top of the command set. It continues until the RETURN command line is encountered.

Use the PARAMETER command line as the first line of a function that expects information from the calling program.

### Caution

A user-defined function must end with a RETURN command line. If you do not pass a value back to the program, or procedure, dBASE IV returns a logical false (.F.) condition.

# GO, GOTO

### Purpose

Moves the record pointer within the datafile.

### Reminder

Think of a record pointer in a datafile as your finger moving through a phone directory. Your finger points to the name and phone number that you selected from the list.

### Command Syntax

**GO/GOTO  BOTTOM/TOP** [IN <*alias*>]

**GO/GOTO** [RECORD] <*record-number*> [IN <*alias*>] <*record-number*>

### Procedures

#### From the Dot Prompt:

1. Open a datafile with the USE command.
2. Type GO 3 and press Enter. The name of the datafile and the record number is displayed on the next line.
3. Then type DISPLAY and press Enter. Record number 3 is shown on the screen.
4. Move to the first record in the datafile by typing GO TOP and pressing Enter. Then display it on the screen.
5. Move the record pointer to the end of the datafile by typing GO BOTTOM and pressing Enter. Display it on the screen.

### From the Control Center:

1. Position the cursor on a file name in the Data column. Press F2 to display the data in a browse screen. Notice the middle section of the status line at the bottom of the screen. A 1 / 4 means that the pointer is positioned on record 1 of 4 in the datafile.

2. Press F10 to access the menu at the top of the screen. Then open the Go To submenu and select the Last Record option. The last record in the datafile is moved to the top of the screen.

3. Access the Go To submenu again. Select the Record Number option. When asked for the record number, type 3 and press Enter. Record number 3 is moved to the top line of the data screen.

### Notes

The record numbers identify the position of the record within the datafile. Records are saved in the same order that they are added to the datafile. Each new record is appended to the end of the open datafile.

Use the INDEX or SORT commands to put the data in other sequences. For example, enter the data as it is available. Then use the INDEX or SORT commands to provide the desired sequence.

### Caution

If you go to the bottom of the datafile (GO BOTTOM) and then issue a SKIP command from the dot prompt, an extra record number is displayed although the record is not there.

# HELP

### Purpose

Views at least one screen of instructions or assistance.

## Reminder

When the F1 function key is pressed, dBASE IV displays the main help menu. Use the arrow keys to position the bounce bar on the desired selection and press Enter.       .

## Command Syntax

**HELP**  [*<dBASE IV keyword>*]

## Procedures

### From the Dot Prompt:

1.  Type HELP at the dot prompt and press Enter. A menu of help options is displayed on the screen.
2.  Press the up- and down-arrow keys to position the bounce bar on the desired option. Then press Enter to open a help window and display information about the selected option.
3.  Press Esc to return to the dot prompt.

### From the Control Center:

1.  Position the bounce bar on one of the Control Center columns.
2.  Press F1 so the first help page appears in a window on your screen.
3.  Use the arrow keys to position the bounce bar on one of the options at the bottom of the window. Press Enter to select it.
4.  Press Esc to return to the Control Center.

## Notes

Pressing F1 at the dot prompt has the same effect as typing HELP.

Provide a specific command on the HELP line to view information for the command.

# IF, ENDIF

## Purpose

Controls the way the data is processed when it meets the specified criteria. For example, if the record is a debit, prints the amount in column A. Otherwise, prints the amount in column B.

## Reminder

Always review the program for loops (DO WHILE or SCAN) that are needed to prevent hard loops. For example, if a loop is established within another loop and the end of file is encountered, you need to exit the outer loop. Use the IF...ENDIF syntax to test for EOF( ) and provide an exit to the loop.

## Command Syntax

IF  <condition>
  <true-commands>
[ELSE
  <false-commands>]
ENDIF

## Procedures

### From the Dot Prompt:

1.  Include the IF, ENDIF command set to perform one set of commands when the condition is true and, optionally, another set of commands when the condition is false. The IF command line specifies the condition. The commands that follow it (true commands) are performed only when the condition is evaluated as true. Then, processing continues with the commands following the ENDIF.

2.  Include the ELSE command line when you need command lines that follow it to be performed when the condition is evaluated as false. Then processing continues with the commands that follow the ENDIF.

3.  At times, you need to include at least one IF,
    ENDIF command set within another. This tech-
    nique is called a "nested" IF. For example, the
    following commands print the subscription years
    for each customer on the report:

```
if num_mos = 12
    @ lncnt,50 say "1 Year"
else
    if num_mos = 24
        @ lncnt,50 say "2 Years"
    else
        @ lncnt,50 say "3 Years"
    endif
endif
```

This command set is "nested" because an IF, ENDIF
command set is enclosed within another IF, ENDIF.
Notice that the set contains two IF command lines and
two matching ENDIF command lines. dBASE IV does
not require the indention of each line, but it is easier to
see that for every IF, there is an ENDIF.

***From the Control Center:***

1.  Use the query capability to establish the special
    conditions for a datafile. Perform several queries, if
    needed, to create the desired datafile.
2.  Set the query and its view so the data is selected
    properly. When the report prints, or a datafile is
    updated, only the data matching the established
    query will be used. ***NOTE***:  This only simulates
    what IF...ENDIF can do.

*Note*

The IF command line specifies the condition. The
ENDIF marks the end of the conditional command set.

*Caution*

An IF always must be used with an ENDIF. Otherwise,
all commands after the IF are treated as part of the true
condition until an ENDIF is encountered or the program
ends.

# IMPORT

### Purpose
Accepts data from other popular software packages. Imports data from RapidFile, dBASE II, Framework II, Lotus 1-2-3, or PFS: FILE. The data is saved in a dBASE IV datafile.

### Reminder
Verify that the datafile to be imported is available on a disk drive. Create the dBASE IV datafile structure that is to receive the data. If the dBASE IV datafile has not been created, one will be created with the same root name as the file being imported.

### Command Syntax
**IMPORT FROM** *<file-name>* [TYPE] **PFS/ DBASEII/FW2/RPD/WK1**

### Procedures
#### From the Dot Prompt:
1. Open the dBASE IV datafile that is to receive the data.
2. At the next dot prompt, type `IMPORT FROM C:\FW\SALES.FW2 TYPE FW2` to import a Framework II file from the FW subdirectory on drive C.
3. Type `USE` to close the dBASE IV datafile and save it onto the disk.

#### From the Control Center:
1. Select the datafile to receive the import.
2. Press F10 to access the menu at the top of the screen. Open the Tools submenu and select the Import option.
3. Use the arrow keys to position the bounce bar on the type of file being imported to dBASE IV and press Enter to select it. A window of the selected type of datafiles appears on your screen.
4. Position the bounce bar on the proper file name and press Enter to select it.

*Note*

If the package that you need to use is not included in the
list of the Import submenu, specify the delimiter and
then select the Text Fixed-length Fields option.

*Caution*

The dBASE IV file structure must be created so the
datafile fields are in the same order as the imported data.
Otherwise, the data may end up in the wrong fields.

# INDEX

*Purpose*

Puts data in an order that makes it easy for you to find
the desired information. For example, a phone directory
is sequenced by last name, first name, and middle initial.

*Reminder*

Determine the sequence that you need to work properly
with the data in the file. For example, when you are
comparing two datafiles that include an equivalent field,
the work is easier when both files are in the same order.

*Command Syntax*

**INDEX  ON**  *<key-expression>*  **TO**  *<index-file-name>*
**/TAG**  *<tag-name>* [OF *<multiple-index-file-name>*]
[UNIQUE] [DESCENDING]

**REINDEX**

*Procedures*

**From the Dot Prompt:**

1.  Open the datafile.
2.  Create an index for the open datafile by using the
    INDEX command. For example, type INDEX ON
    NAME TO CUSTOMER and press Enter.

3. Create a multiple field index by including the concatination (+) symbol between character fields. For example, create an index on state (a character field) and customer number (a numeric field) by issuing the `INDEX ON STATE+STR (CUSTNUM,6,0) TO STCUST` command.

***From the Control Center:***

1. Open a datafile. Press Shift-F2 to display the data structure and move the bounce bar to the menu line at the top of the screen.

2. The Organize submenu is now active. Position the bounce bar on the Create New Index option and press Enter to select it. Another window opens on your screen.

3. Use the options to specify the name of the index, the index expression (key field string), ascending or descending, and whether you want to see duplicate records.

4. Select the Name of Index option. Type the name for the index.

5. Then select the Index Expression option and type the fields to be used to organize the data. For example, type `STATE+NAME` in the input area and press Enter.

6. Because the other options are set to the dBASE IV default values, press Ctrl-End. A window opens to show you the progress of the operation. When it is complete, the datafile structure returns to the screen.

_____

*Notes*

An index file (.NDX) is like the index in the back of a book. Use .NDX files to tell dBASE IV where to go within the datafile (.DBF) to make the records look like they are in sequence.

Indexed datafiles only look like they are in the specified order. The records remain in the order that they were input or sorted.

*Caution*

An index is created for a specific datafile, and dBASE IV reminds you of that fact if you try to use an index that was not created from the open datafile.

# INPUT

*Purpose*

Stops the program activity and asks the user for some information. For example, asks the user for a date range that is used to pull specific data from the datafile.

*Reminder*

The INPUT command is similar to the ACCEPT and WAIT commands.

*Command Syntax*

**INPUT** [*<prompt>*] **TO** *<memvar>*

*Procedures*

***From the Dot Prompt:***

Type `INPUT "Enter the beginning date"`
`TO MFROM` and press Enter. The text within the quotation marks is displayed on the next line, and the cursor is waiting for you to type a value.

***From the Control Center:***

There is no similar capability from the submenus.

*Note*

The INPUT command creates character or numeric variables.

*Caution*

When you use the ACCEPT, INPUT, or WAIT commands, you cannot control the user's response.

# INSERT

### Purpose
Adds records within a datafile instead of to the end.

### Reminder
When using the Control Center, press Ctrl-N to insert a blank record before the record where you have positioned the cursor. Press Ctrl-U to flag records for deletion.

### Command Syntax
INSERT [BEFORE] [BLANK]

### Procedures
#### From the Dot Prompt:
1. Open a datafile.
2. Move the record pointer to a record where you want to insert a new blank record.
3. Insert a blank record by issuing the INSERT command. The screen changes to an APPEND screen for you to type the information into the blank record.

#### From the Control Center:
1. Open a datafile and press F2 to use the Browse screen.
2. Press the down arrow to move to the point of insertion. Press F10 and choose Records/Blank Record to insert a blank record before the current record.

### Note
Include the BEFORE clause in the INSERT command to put the new blank record in front of the current record.

### Caution
If you insert the new record in the wrong place, press Ctrl-U or issue the DELETE command to flag it for deletion. Then use PACK.

# JOIN

## *Purpose*

Combines at least two datafiles.

## *Reminder*

The JOIN command combines all, or selected, fields or records of two datafiles to create a new datafile. For example, JOIN combines customer information with sales transactions.

## *Command Syntax*

**JOIN WITH** *<alias>* **TO** *<file-name>* [FIELDS *<field-list>*] **FOR** *<condition>*

## *Procedures*

### *From the Dot Prompt:*

Open two datafiles in different areas. Then select the primary datafile and issue the JOIN command as shown in the following command lines:

```
SELECT 1
USE CUSTOMER INDEX CUSTOMER
SELECT 2
USE SALES
INDEX ON CUST_NO TO SALES
SELECT 1
JOIN WITH SALES TO TEMP1 FOR
    A-<CUST_NO = B->CUST_NO
```

### *From the Control Center:*

1. Open the primary datafile. Press the right arrow to move the bounce bar to the Create option in the Queries column. Press Enter to select it.
2. Press F10 and select the Add File to Query option from the Layout submenu. When the datafile window opens, select the second datafile for your query.
3. Move the bounce bar to the key field in one of the datafiles.

4. Press F10 and select the Create Link by Pointing option. When the submenu disappears, LINK1 is shown in the selected field.
5. Press F3 to move up or F4 to move down to the other file layout. Position the bounce bar in the key field and press Enter so LINK1 appears in the key field column of both query structures.
6. Use F5 to add or remove fields from each datafile for the view to complete the query definition.
7. Then press F2 to process the query. When the browse screen appears, verify that fields from both datafiles are available.
8. Save the new JOINed datafile on disk.

### Note

Sort or index the datafiles used in the JOIN operation. The order of the records is important because each command compares key field values.

### Caution

Specify the datafile with multiple records for a key value as the primary file. Join the other file to it for a proper datafile.

# LABEL FORM

### Purpose

Prints labels for the open datafile. For example, prints name and address labels for you to mail letters to your customers.

### Reminder

Measure the size of a gum label and the distance between labels.

### Command Syntax

**LABEL FORM** *<label-file-name>*/? [SAMPLE]
[*<scope>*] [FOR *<condition>*] [WHILE *<condition>*]
[TO PRINTER/TO FILE *<file-name>*]

## *Procedures*

### *From the Dot Prompt:*

1. Issue the CREATE LABEL command to define the label format.
2. After the label is saved on disk, issue a LABEL FORM command to see the results of your work. For example, `LABEL FORM CUST1` sends the customer address labels to the screen. Because the screen is not as large as the paper, the information scrolls off the screen unless you press Ctrl-S to stop and start the information as you review it.
3. Send the label to the printer by including the TO PRINT clause in the LABEL FORM command. For example, `LABEL FORM CUST1 TO PRINT` sends the labels to the printer as well as the screen.

### *From the Control Center:*

1. Open the datafile; create and save the label form.
2. If the label form is already on disk, position the bounce bar on the option in the Labels column. Select the Print Label option from the open window.

## *Note*

Adjust the distance between labels by selecting the Spaces Between Label Columns option from the Dimensions submenu.

## *Caution*

Some label forms are not designed for computer printers (you should purchase labels, as well as any special form, that are spaced according to normal printer guidelines).

# ═ LIST ═══════════════════════════

## *Purpose*

Sends information to the screen, printer, or disk file.

*Reminder*

The LIST and DISPLAY commands perform nearly the same function. Use either command to view information. Changes are not allowed when you're using these commands.

*Command Syntax*

LIST/DISPLAY [[FIELDS] <*expression-list*>] [OFF]
[<*scope*>] [FOR <*condition*>] [WHILE <*condition*>]
[TO PRINTER/TO FILE <*file-name*>]

LIST/DISPLAY FILES [LIKE <*skeleton*>] [TO
PRINTER/TO FILE <*file-name*>]

LIST/DISPLAY HISTORY [LAST <*expN*>] [TO
PRINTER/TO FILE <*file-name*>]

LIST/DISPLAY STATUS/MEMORY
[TO PRINTER/TO FILE <*file-name*>]

LIST/DISPLAY STRUCTURE [IN <*alias*>] [TO
PRINTER/TO FILE <*file-name*>]

LIST/DISPLAY USERS

*Procedures*

*From the Dot Prompt:*

1. Open a datafile. Type LIST and press Enter. All records in the file scroll up the screen. If the record length is longer than 80 positions across, the information wraps to the next line.

2. Type DISPLAY ALL and press Enter. The same screen appears as in step 1, but when the screen fills, scrolling stops and you are asked to press any key to continue.

3. Type GO TOP and press Enter to return to the first record in the datafile. Then issue the DISPLAY command with a field name. For example, DISPLAY NAME presents the record number and name of the first record. The name in only the first record is displayed.

4. Type `LIST NAME` and press Enter. Just the NAME field for all records is listed.

5. Type `DISPLAY STATUS` and press Enter. The first screen shows the datafile in use as well as the environment status. The other screens show the rest of the environment status.

6. Press Enter until the dot prompt returns on the screen.

7. Type `LIST STRUCTURE` and press Enter. The structure of the open datafile is displayed on the screen.

***From the Control Center:***

1. Position the bounce bar on the datafile and press Enter.

2. A window of options opens on your screen. Your choices are to Use File, Modify Structure/Order, or Display Data. Select the Display Data option.

3. Use the Browse screen to review and/or change the data.

4. Press Esc to return to the Control Center screen without saving the changes.

---

*Notes*

Use the LIST/DISPLAY FILES command like the DIR command.

Type `DISPLAY HISTORY` to see the last several commands issued from the dot prompt.

---

*Caution*

A LIST and DISPLAY ALL command leaves the record pointer on the last record in the datafile. Use the GO command to return to the top of the file before issuing another LIST command.

# LOAD

---

*Purpose*

Reads a binary program from the disk into memory.

### Reminder

You must read the program from disk into memory with the LOAD command. Run the program by issuing a CALL command. Then remove it from memory with the RELEASE MODULE command.

### Command Syntax

LOAD <binary-file-name>

### Procedures

**From the Dot Prompt:**

Issue the LOAD command to read the binary program from the disk.

**From the Control Center:**

There is no similar capability from the Control Center.

### Note

You must read the non-dBASE IV program from disk with the LOAD command before you can run it with the CALL command.

### Caution

When it is no longer needed, always remove the dBASE IV program from computer memory. Otherwise, you may experience an "Out of Memory" error while running an application.

# LOCATE

### Purpose

Looks through the open file for a specific value in at least one field.

### Reminder

Use the LOCATE command for any file. Sorted or indexed data does not influence the LOCATE command. If the record found is not the one you want, resume the search by issuing a CONTINUE command.

*Command Syntax*

   LOCATE  [FOR] *<condition-1>* [*<scope>*] [WHILE
      *<condition-2>*]

   CONTINUE

*Procedures*

   ### From the Dot Prompt:

   1.  Open the datafile with or without its index file.
   2.  Issue a LOCATE command. For example, type
       `LOCATE FOR ZIPCODE = "70134"` and
       press Enter. When the dot prompt returns, display
       the record to verify the result of the search.
   3.  Find the next record matching the condition by
       issuing the CONTINUE command.
   4.  Repeat the CONTINUE, DISPLAY process until
       you encounter the proper record or the end of the
       file.

   ### From the Control Center:

   1.  Open the datafile. Press Enter to move the bounce
       bar to the field you want to search.
   2.  Press F10 to access the menu at the top of the
       screen. Then move right to the Go To option.
   3.  Press the down arrow to position the bounce bar on
       the Forward Search option and press Enter.
   4.  When asked for the search string, type it in the
       input area and press Enter. If found, the submenus
       are removed and the bounce bar is positioned on the
       requested record.

*Notes*

   Use the SET EXACT command to consider or ignore
   case.

   Use the SET NEAR command to find the specified
   value or its nearest match rather than an end-of-file
   condition.

   Test for an end-of-file condition because the EOF( )
   function returns a True condition.

From the dot prompt, use the following examples for specifying search criteria for the different data type fields:

```
Character    "SUSAN"
Numeric      73728
Date         DTOC(SUB_DATE)
```

Use a memory variable to provide a changeable search value.

### Caution
The LOCATE command is slower than the FIND or SEEK commands.

# LOGOUT

### Purpose
Ends the current session and returns to the sign-on screen from a dBASE IV application when you are using dBASE IV on a network system.

### Reminder
Write or change the dBASE IV main menu program to include an option to end the dBASE IV session. When the user selects the menu option, the user is logged off of the network.

### Command Syntax
LOGOUT

### Procedures
#### From the Dot Prompt:
Insert the LOGOUT command in the network main menu of the application program. When this command is encountered, it ends the application, as well as the workstation session.

### *From the Control Center:*
There is no similar capability available from the Control Center.

### *Note*
Issue the PROTECT command when beginning the dBASE IV session. This procedure establishes the log-in verification functions and sets the user access level.

### *Caution*
If the PROTECT command was not used during the dBASE IV session, the user is returned to the dot prompt rather than the log-in screen.

# MODIFY APPLICATION

See **CREATE APPLICATION**

# MODIFY COMMAND/FILE

### *Purpose*
Used to write or change a dBASE IV program.

### *Reminder*
Write custom programs to be used with the programs produced with the Applications Generator.

### *Command Syntax*
**MODIFY COMMAND/FILE** *<file-name>*
  [WINDOW *<window-name>*]

### *Procedures*
#### *From the Dot Prompt:*
1. Issue the MODIFY COMMAND from the dot prompt and press Enter. For example, type
   `MODIFY COMMAND TEST1` and press Enter.

2. Press the PgDn, PgUp, Home, and End keys to move the cursor through the program. If you have made changes, save them by pressing Ctrl-W. Otherwise, press Ctrl-Q.

3. Run the program by issuing the DO command.

*From the Control Center:*

There is no equivalent capability from the submenus.

---

*Notes*

If the program does not exist, a blank screen is available for you to type the new program. Otherwise, it is displayed on the screen.

Always write programs that close the open datafiles as soon as possible. This technique helps you avoid datafile problems.

---

*Caution*

If you try to create a program with a name that already exists on disk, dBASE IV accesses the existing file as if you typed MODIFY COMMAND.

# MODIFY LABEL

See CREATE LABEL

# MODIFY QUERY/VIEW

See CREATE QUERY/VIEW

# MODIFY REPORT

See CREATE REPORT

# MODIFY SCREEN

See **CREATE SCREEN**

# MODIFY STRUCTURE

See **CREATE STRUCTURE**

# MOVE WINDOW

See **DEFINE WINDOW**

# NOTE

### *Purpose*

Provides information to anyone who reviews the application program. For example, describes its name and purpose.

Also, uses program documentation to describe complicated sections of commands. For example, documents the section of commands that perform a series of calculations.

### *Reminder*

Include documentation to coding in a dBASE IV program.

### *Command Syntax*

NOTE/* *<text>*

[*<command>*] **&&** *<text>*

## Procedures

### From the Dot Prompt:

The dBASE IV sample program lines open the SALES
data and index files. It ignores all comment lines.
Review the use of the documentation commands in the
following program lines:

```
*****************************************
*   MENU.PRG - PROVIDES A BOUNCE BAR   *
*       MENU FOR THE SALES SYSTEM      *
*          NOTE: copyright 1989        *
*****************************************

USE SALES INDEX SALES &&open the
  &&datafile in customer # order
```

### From the Control Center:

There is no equivalent capability from the Control
Center submenus.

## Notes

Use the double ampersand (&&) to indicate that what
follows the && on the line is information rather than
commands.

Issue the NOTE command and asterisk symbol (*) at the
beginning of a program command line.

Use the && symbols to provide documentation after a
command. dBASE IV performs the command and
ignores everything after the && symbols.

## Caution

If you put comment information on a command line, you
must precede the information with the && command.

# ═| ON ERROR, ESCAPE, KEY |═

## *Purpose*

Traps errors or recognizes certain keys encountered while the program is running.

## *Reminder*

Write a program. Then identify all problem situations that the user may encounter while using it. Next, change the program to recognize and respond to each problem. Test the program to verify that it runs properly. Finally, have a user test your application before putting it into production. Because you know which keys to press, your test is seldom as complete as a user test.

## *Command Syntax*

ON ERROR/ESCAPE  [*<commands>*]

ON KEY  [LABEL *<key-label-name>*] [*<commands>*]

## *Procedures*

### *From the Dot Prompt:*

1. Include the ON ERROR command at the beginning of the program. If an error occurs, the command, procedure, or function included in the command line is performed immediately. For example, ON ERROR DO ERRORMSG tells dBASE IV to perform the ERRORMSG procedure when an error occurs during the application.

2. Use the ON ESCAPE command to identify a command, procedure, or function to be performed when the user presses the Esc key. Display a message to tell the user about the Esc option so the user is aware of the option. For example, include the ON ESCAPE DO ABORT_IT command line in the application to perform the ABORT_IT procedure when the user presses Esc.

3. Include the ON KEY command to specify a key and a procedure or program to be performed when the

user presses the key included in the command line.
Specify the key except the Esc key in this
command.

***From the Control Center:***
There is no equivalent capability available from the
submenus.

_____
*Notes*

Include these commands in the beginning of the
program to set the trap. It is not processed unless the
situation occurs while the application is running.

When you set an ON condition, it remains in effect until
another of the same ON condition occurs.

Turn off an ON condition by specifying the ON
command without a command or procedure name.

_____
*Caution*

If the command line refers to a procedure, the procedure
must properly handle the error.

# ON PAD

_____
*Purpose*

Identifies a pop-up menu associated with the menu
option.

_____
*Reminder*

When the user selects the option from the menu, the
proper pop-up menu is displayed on the screen. It is like
a submenu for the menu option.

_____
*Command Syntax*
    ON  PAD  *<pad-name>*  OF  *<menu-name>*
      [ACTIVATE POPUP *<popup-name>*]

## Procedures

### From the Dot Prompt:

1. Combine the DEFINE MENU, DEFINE PAD, DEFINE POPUP, and DEFINE BAR commands to define the menu (vertical) and submenus (pop-up).

2. Include the ON PAD command line to identify the pop-up menu associated with the menu option. When the user selects an option that matches an ON PAD command line, the proper pop-up submenu is activated automatically.

### From the Control Center:

The Applications Generator automatically handles menu operation.

## Note

Use bounce bar menus as often as possible to prevent the user from having to type. Checking for a valid user response is unnecessary.

## Caution

Include the RELEASE POPUPS command in the program to remove the menu definition from memory. Otherwise, you may experience an "Out of Memory" error while running an application.

# =| ON PAGE |═══════════ ─────────── ══

## Purpose

Identifies a command or string of commands to perform when a specified line on a printed page has been reached.

## Reminder

Identify the line number and information to be printed.

## Command Syntax

ON PAGE [AT LINE <expN> <commands>]

*Procedures*

*From the Dot Prompt:*

1. Include the ON PAGE command line before the SET DEVICE TO PRINT, or SET PRINT ON command line. For example, issue `ON PAGE AT LINE 2 DO HEADER1`. Each page is printed with the information from the HEADER procedure.

2. Issue an ON PAGE command without the optional clauses to disengage the page handler.

*From the Control Center:*

There is no equivalent capability available from the Control Center screen.

*Notes*

Include this command in the beginning of the program to set the trap. It is not processed unless the printer is activated.

When you set an ON PAGE command, it remains in effect until another ON PAGE is encountered.

*Caution*

If the command line refers to a procedure, the procedure must properly handle the error.

# ON READERROR

*Purpose*

Traps errors that occur during data entry.

*Reminder*

Include the ON READERROR command to trap errors that occur during full-screen operations. Specify a procedure that handles the error situation. For example, validate the input to a field that must fall within an acceptable range.

*Command Syntax*
   **ON READERROR** [*<commands>*]

*Procedures*
   ***From the Dot Prompt:***
   Include the ON READERROR command in programs
   that edit the datafile. For example, set the ON
   READERROR command to validate the input to a field
   that must fall within an acceptable range.
   ***From the Control Center:***
   There is no equivalent capability available from the
   Control Center.

*Notes*
   The trap is not processed unless the situation occurs
   while you're running the application.

   When you set an ON READERROR condition, it
   remains in effect until another ON READERROR
   command is encountered.

   Turn off an ON condition by specifying the ON
   command without a command or procedure name.

*Caution*
   If the command line refers to a procedure, the procedure
   must properly handle the error.

═══╡ # ON SELECTION PAD ╞═══════

   See **DEFINE MENU**

═══╡ # ON SELECTION POPUP ╞═══

   See **DEFINE POPUP**

# PACK

See **DELETE**

# PARAMETERS

### *Purpose*

Passes values from programs or procedures to procedures or functions for additional processing and often returns new values to the originating program or procedure.

### *Reminders*

A procedure is a set of commands that are performed at least twice from a program so repeating a set of commands is unnecessary.

A function is identified by the FUNCTION command as the first line and the RETURN( ) command as the last line. The RETURN( ) command line must send information back to the calling program or procedure.

### *Command Syntax*

PARAMETERS  *<parameter-list>*

### *Procedures*

#### *From the Dot Prompt:*

1.  Write a program that includes a procedure or function that requires information from a calling procedure. For example, the Headers procedure in the following command lines uses a function called Centered. The procedure sends the width of the page and the value to be centered on that page as parameters. The function includes the PARAMETERS command to accept the information from the calling procedure:

```
procedure headers
lncnt = 5
@ lncnt,01 say date(  )
mtemp = "ABC MAIL-OUT COMPANY"
@ lncnt,centered(80,mtemp) say
mtemp
@ lncnt,70 say "Page"
pagecnt = pagecnt + 1
@ lncnt,75 say pagecnt pict "999"
lncnt = lncnt + 1
mtemp = "Subscription Report for
"+dtoc(mfrom)+" thru "+dtoc(mto)
@ lncnt,centered(80,mtemp) say
mtemp
lncnt = lncnt + 3
@ lncnt,10 say "Name"
@ lncnt,35 say "Phone #"
lncnt = lncnt + 3
return

function centered( )
parameters mcols, mvalue
mnum = ((mcols-len(mvalue))/2)
return(mnum)
```

2.  The procedure passes the report width of 80 and the
    value to be positioned to the CENTERED( )
    function. It calculates and returns the column
    position needed to center the value across the page.

***From the Control Center:***

There is no equivalent capability from the Control
Center.

---

***Note***

Use the PARAMETER command line as the first line of
a procedure or function that expects information from
the calling program.

---

***Caution***

A user-defined function must end with a RETURN
command line. If you do not pass a value back to the

program, or procedure, dBASE IV gives an
error message.

# PLAY MACRO

### *Purpose*

Performs a macro that is being held in memory.

### *Reminder*

Use the RESTORE MACROS command to read the
macros from disk.

### *Command Syntax*

PLAY MACRO *<macro-name>*

### *Procedures*

#### *From the Dot Prompt:*

Include the RESTORE and PLAY commands in
programs that use macros. The RESTORE command
reads the specified file of macros from the disk. To play
the macro, issue the PLAY command.

#### *From the Control Center:*

1. Select the Load Library option from the Tools/
   Macros submenus.
2. Play the macro by pressing Alt-F10 and press the
   key that you assigned the macro held in memory.

### *Note*

All macros are created through the Control Center. Use
the Begin Recording and End Recording options from
the Tools/Macros submenu to start and stop the
recording activity.

### *Caution*

If you restore a macro file that includes key assignments
that already exist in memory, the new macro definition
replaces the existing macro.

# PRINTJOB/ENDPRINTJOB

### *Purpose*

Controls printing activity. Use it to send print codes
(type fonts), eject a page, initialize, and activate dBASE
IV system memory variables used to print a report.

### *Reminder*

Write a program to print a report. Use the ?, ??, or
@...SAY commands to create the output for the printer.

### *Command Syntax*

**PRINTJOB**

   *<commands>*
**ENDPRINTJOB**

### *Procedures*

#### *From the Dot Prompt:*

Include the PRINTJOB command set in a report
program. The format for the command set follows: The
PRINTJOB command line identifies the starting point
for the report. The ENDPRINTJOB command line
identifies the ending point. All command lines between
the PRINTJOB and ENDPRINTJOB commands are
processed as part of the printjob set. For example, the
following set of command lines sets the number of
copies and prints the report twice:

```
_pcopies = 2
printjob
do while .not. eof()
   if lncnt > 55
      lncnt = 5
      @ lncnt,01 say date()
      @ lncnt,35 say "ABC
        MAIL-OUT COMPANY"
      @ lncnt,70 say "Page"
```

```
        pagecnt = pagecnt + 1
        @ lncnt,75 say pagecnt
           pict "999"
      lncnt = lncnt + 1
      @ lncnt,22 say "Subscription
         Report for";
      "+dtoc(mfrom)+" thru
      "+dtoc(mto)
      lncnt = lncnt + 3
      @ lncnt,10 say "Name"
      @ lncnt,35 say "Phone #"
      lncnt = lncnt + 3
   endif
   if sub_date >= mfrom .and.
      sub_date <= mto
      @ lncnt,01 say name
      @ lncnt,32 say phone_1
   endif
    skip
   enddo
      endprintjob
```

***From the Control Center:***

This capability is automatically provided when printing
a report from the Report column of the Control Center.

---

*Note*

Report forms include the printjob capabilities
automatically. Set the number of copies (_pcopies)
before issuing the REPORT FORM command. Page
ejection responds to the setting of _pscodes, _pecodes,
and _peject.

---

*Caution*

Do not include a PRINTJOB command set within
another printjob. dBASE IV does not allow such
"nesting" activity.

# PRIVATE

## *Purpose*

Identifies private memory variables and arrays that are
to be available only to the program that created them or
to the programs run by that program.

Uses PUBLIC to identify variables and arrays that are
created and used throughout the application until
RELEASE or QUIT is encountered.

## *Reminder*

Identify the information that needs to be held in memory
so the program runs properly. For example, specify a
variable as private when it is used to verify a password.

## *Command Syntax*

**PRIVATE  ALL**  [LIKE/EXCEPT <*skeleton*>]

**PRIVATE**  <*memvar-list*>/[ARRAY <*array-definition-
list*>]

**PUBLIC**  <*memory-variable-list*>/[ARRAY <*array-
definition-list*>]

## *Procedures*

### *From the Dot Prompt:*

1. Use the following command lines to create private
   memory variables called mname and mnum:

   ```
   * TEST1.PRG - A sample program to
     test private memory variables.
   *
   private mname,mnum
   mname = "Jerry"
   mnum = 9
   ```

2. Use the PUBLIC command if the variables are
   needed throughout the application:

   ```
   * TEST1.PRG - A sample program to
     test private memory variables.
   ```

```
*
public mname,mnum
mname = "Jerry"
mnum = 9
```

### *From the Control Center:*

There is no equivalent capability from the Control
Center submenus.

---

### *Notes*

When the program that created the private memory
variables and arrays has completed its run, its private
memory variables are released immediately.

Public variables and arrays are available at any time, to
any program, while you are running the application.
Private variables and arrays are available only to the
current and programs run by the current program that
created them.

---

### *Caution*

When a variable or array is declared as public, its value
can be changed by any program.

# PROCEDURE

---

### *Purpose*

Writes a program in sections to perform specialized
tasks.

---

### *Reminder*

A procedure file contains several programs. A program
that uses procedure files runs faster than one that uses
separate programs.

---

### *Command Syntax*

**PROCEDURE** *<procedure-name>*

## Procedures

### From the Dot Prompt:

1. Use the PROCEDURE command to identify small programs called by a main program. Include the PARAMETERS command line in a program or procedure to accept information from the calling program.

2. Issue the DO command to perform a procedure. For example, the following procedure (called headers) sets the line counter and prints all the heading information:

```
procedure headers
  lncnt = 5
  @ lncnt,01 say date()
  @ lncnt,35 say "ABC MAIL-OUT
    COMPANY"
  @ lncnt,70 say "Page"
    pagecnt = pagecnt + 1
  @ lncnt,75 say pagecnt pict
   "999"
    lncnt = lncnt + 1
  @ lncnt,22 say "Subscription
    Report for";
    +dtoc(mfrom)+"thru"+dtoc(mto)
  lncnt = lncnt + 3
  @ lncnt,10 say "Name"
  @ lncnt,35 say "Phone #"
  lncnt = lncnt + 3
  return
```

### From the Control Center:

There is no equivalent capability from the Control Center.

### Notes

Issue a SET PROCEDURE command to open or close a procedure.

Use the PARAMETER command line as the first line of a procedure or function that expects information from the calling program.

### Caution
A procedure must end with a RETURN command line.

# PROTECT

### Purpose
Restricts access to dBASE IV, datafiles, or fields in any of the following three ways:

| | |
|---|---|
| Log-in | provides access to dBASE IV to authorized personnel only |
| File and/or Field | authorizes access to certain files, and/or fields of dBASE IV files |
| Data Encryption | changes all data within the protected file so that unauthorized users cannot read it |

### Reminder
Use this capability to restrict access to authorized users only. For example, a data-entry clerk does not need access (for viewing or changes) to employee salary information. Therefore, authorize the clerk to access only name, address, and social security number. Password-protect the employee salary field.

### Command Syntax
PROTECT

### Procedures
#### From the Dot Prompt:
1. Issue the PROTECT command line to access its submenus.
2. Type and verify the database administrator's password.
3. Use the Users submenu to assign the following user protection information: Login Name, Password, Group Name, Full Name, Access Level, Store User Profile, Delete User from Group. This information determines which users may start dBASE IV.

4.  Change to the Files submenu to provide the following information: New File, Group Name, File Access Privileges, Field Access Privileges, Access Level, Establish Field Privileges, Store File Privileges, Cancel Current Entry. This information determines which users have access to data and whether they can only read data or make changes also.
5.  Open the Reports submenu to review user security levels.
6.  When all protection activity is complete, use the Exit submenu to Save, Abandon, or Exit the protection menus and return to the dot prompt.

***From the Control Center:***
1.  Press F10 to access the menu at the top of the screen.
2.  Choose Tools/Protect Data.
3.  Follow steps 2 through 6 to make protection changes.

***Note***

Use any combination of protection schemes to limit access of sensitive data to authorized users only.

***Caution***

When a password is assigned, it is recorded in a DBSYSTEM.DB file. This file is encrypted automatically to prevent unauthorized access.

# PUBLIC

See **PRIVATE**

# QUIT

***Purpose***

Ends the current dBASE IV session.

## *Reminder*

All open datafiles are closed before you exit to the operating system.

## *Command Syntax*

QUIT

## *Procedures*

### *From the Dot Prompt:*

Type QUIT and press Enter.

### *From the Control Center:*

1. Press F10 to access the menu line at the top of the screen.
2. Select the Quit to DOS option from the Exit submenu.

## *Note*

When you write dBASE IV applications that are used by inexperienced people, provide a way for them to end the session when they have completed their work. Otherwise, they might turn off the computer before all changed files are saved on disk.

## *Caution*

You often lose open dBASE IV datafiles, programs, etc. by turning off the computer without closing them. The most reliable way of keeping your work is to end the current session.

Although you can use QUIT to close all open data files, a better procedure is to issue the USE or CLOSEDATABASES command prior to issuing QUIT.

# READ

See @ SAY, GET.

# RECALL

## *Purpose*

Removes the deletion flag for records in a database.

## *Reminder*

If no records are flagged for deletion, this command does not affect the datafile.

## *Command Syntax*

RECALL [*<scope>*] [FOR *<condition>*] [WHILE *<condition>*]

## *Procedures*

### *From the Dot Prompt:*

1. Open a datafile. Use the GO command to move to the record you want to recall.
2. Display the record to see that the current record is the correct one. The asterisk (*) between the record number and the first field value identifies this record for removal.
3. Type RECALL and press Enter. You are told that one record is recalled (unmarked). Display the record to verify the result.

### *From the Control Center:*

1. Open a datafile and press F2 to use the Browse screen.
2. Move the bounce bar to the deleted record in the datafile.
3. Press F10 to access the menu line at the top of the screen. Select Clear Deletion Mark to unmark the current record.
4. Select the Exit option from the Exit submenu to return to the Control Center.

## *Notes*

Use RECALL ALL to unmark all records flagged for deletion.

Limit the effect of the RECALL command by specifying
a condition. For example, `RECALL ALL FOR
STATE = "CA"` from the dot prompt recalls all
records that contain "CA" in the state field.

# REINDEX

See **INDEX**

# RELEASE

### *Purpose*

Releases the memory variables, modules, menus, popups, and windows that are held in memory.

### *Reminder*

As you define and hold information in memory, the
application processes slower. Free memory as often as
possible.

### *Command Syntax*

**RELEASE** *<memvar-list>*

**RELEASE ALL** [LIKE/EXCEPT *<skeleton>*]

**RELEASE MODULE** [*<module-name-list>*]
/**MENUS** [*<menu-name-list>*]/**POPUPS** [*<popup-
name-list>*]/**WINDOW** [*<window-name-list>*]

### *Procedures*

#### *From the Dot Prompt:*

1. Use RELEASE ALL to free up all the memory used
   by memory variables.
2. Use RELEASE MENUS to free up the memory
   used by pop-up menus.
3. Use RELEASE POPUPS to free up the memory
   used by pop-up menus.

4. Use RELEASE WINDOWS to free up all memory used by windows.

***From the Control Center:***

There is no equivalent capability from the submenus.

---

***Note***

Use the wild card symbol (*) in the LIKE clause of the RELEASE ALL command. For example, `RELEASE ALL LIKE k*` releases all memory variables that have a K as the first letter.

When releasing MENUS, POPUPS, or WINDOWS, you may list the individual name(s) to release.

---

***Caution***

Include the RELEASE command in the program to remove the menu definition from memory. Otherwise, you may experience an "Out of Memory" error while running an application.

# RENAME

---

***Purpose***

Changes the name of files on your disk without ending the dBASE IV session.

---

***Reminder***

You should make sure that the file you want to rename is closed by issuing the USE or CLOSE DATA command.

---

***Command Syntax***

**RENAME** *<old-file-name>* **TO** *<new-file-name>*

---

***Procedures***

***From the Dot Prompt:***

Issue the RENAME command. For example, `RENAME SALES.DBF TO SALES201.DBF` changes the datafile called SALES to SALES201.

### *From the Control Center:*
1. Press F10 to access the menu line at the top of the screen.
2. Select the Tools/DOS Utilities options. A window that contains file names, lengths, date, time, attributes, and space used appears on your screen. Press F10 so a new menu line and a window of submenu options are included on the screen.
3. Position the bounce bar on the file to be renamed.
4. Open the Operations submenu and select the Rename option. When asked for the new name, type it in the input area.

### *Note*
Always specify the file extensions when renaming files.

### *Caution*
If the new file name exists on the specified disk, dBASE IV gives a "File already exists" error message.

# REPLACE

### *Purpose*
Changes the information in a field for at least one record in the open datafile.

### *Reminder*
Open or select a datafile and decide which fields are to be changed during the process.

### *Command Syntax*
REPLACE *<field-name>* WITH *<exp-1>*
    [ADDITIVE] [,*<field-name-2>* WITH *<exp-2>*
    [ADDITIVE] ...] [*<scope>*] [FOR *<condition>*]
    [WHILE *<condition>*]

### *Procedures*
#### *From the Dot Prompt:*
1. Open the datafile (with or without specifying an

index file) in the USE command line.

2. In this example, change the customer number (C) of the current record so it has zeros in the first two of five positions:

```
REPLACE CUST_NO WITH "00" +
SUBSTR(CUST_NO,3,3)
```

3. To change all values in the MTD_SALES (month-to-date sales figures) field to zero, use the following command as follows:

```
REPLACE ALL MTD_SALES WITH 0
```

4. Limit the number of replacements by including a conditional clause. For example, replace all the STATE fields containing "CALIF" with a "CA" value as follows:

```
REPLACE ALL STATE WITH "CA" FOR
STATE = "CALIF"
```

5. Change the values of several fields in a record by stringing them on one line. Separate each field as shown in the following command line. The mName, mCity, and mState are memory variables that contain the new values:

```
REPLACE NAME WITH mName, CITY WITH
mCity, STATE WITH mState
```

### From the Control Center:

1. Open the datafile.
2. Select the Create option from the Queries column.
3. Remove the view by pressing F5.
4. Press F10 and select the Specify Update option from the Update submenu. Another submenu window opens on the screen. Select the Replace Values option. When the submenus disappear, "Replace" is supplied in the first column of the query line.
5. Press Tab to move to the column you want to replace with other values and type the condition. For example, move to the STATE field and type WITH "CA".

6. Reopen the Update submenu and select Perform the Query.

## Note

When two datafiles with the same field name are open during a replace operation, specify the work area by letter (A, B, C,...) or alias name. For example, REPLACE B->CITY WITH A->CITY tells dBASE IV to move the value of the CITY field in the area 1 datafile to the CITY field in the area 2 datafile.

## Caution

When values are replaced in the datafile, the only way to return the data to its original values is by using BEGIN/END TRANSACTION and ROLLBACK. Test new update queries or programs on a copy of the original until you know that the query provides the desired results.

# REPORT FORM

## Purpose

Reports on information contained in your dBASE IV databases. Reports can be columnar, special forms, or mailmerge documents.

## Reminder

The data from your report can come from several databases. Use indexes to sort and arrange the information before running your report.

## Command Syntax

REPORT FORM  *<report-form-file-name>* /?
  [PLAIN] [HEADING *<expC>*] [NOEJECT]
  [SUMMARY] [*<scope>*] [FOR *<condition>*]
  [WHILE *<condition>*] [TO PRINTER/TO FILE
  *<file-name>*]

## Procedures

### From the Dot Prompt:

1. Open the datafiles that are required by the report format.
2. Issue the REPORT FORM command and press Enter. The report is displayed on the screen.
3. Send the report to the printer by including the TO PRINT clause. Each record from the database is printed on paper.

### From the Control Center

1. Open the datafiles needed by the report form.
2. Position the bounce bar on the Report Form option of the Reports column and press Enter. Select the Print Report option.
3. Another window of print options is opened on the screen. Select the Begin Printing option to send the information to the printer.

## Notes

Use the FOR and WHILE clauses to limit the records printed on the report.

Use the NOEJECT option to combine several reports on the same page.

## Caution

Turn on the printer before issuing the REPORT FORM command with a TO PRINT clause.

# RESET

## Purpose

Updates a datafile and can remove the changes you made with the ROLLBACK command.

## Reminder

Identify the necessary processing to be changed before using the RESET command.

## Command Syntax
   RESET [IN <*alias*>]

## Procedures
   ### From the Dot Prompt:
   1. Write a datafile processing program that includes the BEGIN TRANSACTION, END TRANSACTION command set.
   2. Include the BEGIN TRANSACTION command line to identify the starting point for the transaction processing. The END TRANSACTION command marks the end.
   3. Use the ROLLBACK command to restore the database file to its pre-transaction state.
   4. Use the RESET command line to tag the files involved in transaction processing. RESET marks the file when processing begins and is removed upon completion of the procedure or when the ROLLBACK command is used.

   ### From the Control Center:
   There is no equivalent method from the control center.

## Note
   The ROLLBACK command is effective for the APPEND, BROWSE, CHANGE, DELETE, EDIT, RECALL, REPLACE, and UPDATE commands. Also, create new files by using the COPY, CREATE, IMPORT FROM, INDEX, JOIN, SET CATALOG, SORT, and TOTAL commands. Overwriting files or closing open files is not allowed if you intend to use the rollback capability.

## Caution
   Do not include the CLEAR ALL, CLOSE, DELETE FILE, ERASE, INSERT, MODIFY STRUCTURE, PACK, RENAME, or ZAP commands in transaction processing.

# RESTORE

### Purpose

Restores memory variables, macros, and windows from disk files.

### Reminder

Use the SAVE command to write the information in memory onto disk to be used again at a later time. For example, define several windows, save them on disk, and restore them as needed by the application.

### Command Syntax

RESTORE FROM <file-name> [ADDITIVE]

RESTORE MACROS FROM <macro-file>

RESTORE WINDOW <window-name-list> /ALL
  FROM <file-name>

### Procedures

#### From the Dot Prompt:

1. Save memory variables to a file with the command SAVE TO <file-name>. Restore them with the RESTORE FROM <file-name> command.
2. Issue one of the RESTORE commands to read information from disk into memory.

#### From the Control Center:

1. Use the Load Library option from the Tools/Macros submenus to read a macro file from disk.
2. Play the macro by pressing Alt-F10 and press or type the key that you assigned the recorded macro.

### Note

Instead of redefining windows each time, create, and save them once and restore them as needed by the application.

## Caution

If you restore a macro file that includes key assignments that already exist in memory, the new macro definition replaces the existing macro.

# RESUME

## Purpose

Causes suspended programs to resume execution where they were suspended.

## Reminder

When you suspend a program, you can examine database records and memory variables to assist in debugging programs. The RESUME command causes the program to continue execution.

## Command Syntax

RESUME

## Procedures

### From the Dot Prompt:

1. Include the SUSPEND command in a program to temporarily stop the program. The dot prompt is available for you to display or change memory variables, datafile records, or any combination of information.

2. When ready to continue the program as though it had not been stopped, use the RESUME command from the dot prompt. The program continues running each command.

### From the Control Center:

These commands are for programs only. Equivalent capabilities do not exist from the Control Center.

## Note

All memory variables, files, etc. are available after processing the SUSPEND command. Use the ? and

DISPLAY commands to see the values of variables
and fields.

### Caution
Remove all debugging commands before making the
program available to the users.

# RETRY

### Purpose
Retries executing a program that dBASE IV determined
has an error.

### Reminders
The RETRY command is usually included in an error
recovery program.

If an error is encountered when you run a program,
dBASE IV opens a window that identifies the invalid
command with a brief description of the problem unless
you have specified an ON ERROR.

### Command Syntax
**RETRY**

### Procedures
#### From the Dot Prompt:
Include the ON ERROR DO <*file-name*> WITH
ERROR( ) command to handle errors encountered after
the command. The RETRY command tells dBASE IV to
try the  command again.

```
ON ERROR DO FIXIT WITH ERROR( )
USE AFILE

*FIXIT.PRG
PARAMETERS Error
IF Error = 3
  CLOSE DATABASE
```

```
ENDIF
RETRY
```

### *From the Control Center:*
This command is for programs only. Equivalent capabilities do not exist from the Control Center.

### *Note*
Use the RETRY command after issuing a command that needs the printer if the printer had not been turned on.

### *Caution*
Remove all debugging commands before making the program available to the user.

# RETURN

### *Purpose*
Stops a program and returns to the calling program or dot prompt. If the user leaves a required input area blank, for example, a message about the error is displayed, and control is returned to the menu program.

### *Reminder*
Use the RETURN command to stop processing the current program.

### *Command Syntax*
RETURN [<*expression*>/TO MASTER/TO <*procedure*>]

### *Procedures*
#### *From the Dot Prompt:*
1. Review the following command syntax for the RETURN command:

```
Mfrom = Date( )
Mto = Date( )
USE subscrpt INDEX subscrpt
```

```
@ 08,15 TO 14,60 DOUBLE COLOR R/W
@ 09,16 FILL TO 13,59 COLOR W/N
@ 10,20 SAY "Enter the beginning
date " GET Mfrom PICTURE "99/99/
   99"
@ 12,20 SAY "Enter the ending date
" GET Mto PICTURE "99/99/99"
READ
IF Mto - Mfrom > 366
    @ 21,01 SAY "The date range is
    longer than one year -
    aborting the request..."
    WAIT
  RETURN
ENDIF
```

2. Use the RETURN command to cause the current program to send control back to the program or dot prompt that ran the program containing this command.

***From the Control Center:***

This command is for programs only. Equivalent capabilities do not exist from the Control Center.

---

*Notes*

Include the RETURN command (without the optional clauses) at the end of every program to identify the last program line.

If the RETURN command is encountered without the optional clauses, the processing of the current program ends. Processing resumes with the program that called that program, after the line that made the call.

When the [TO MASTER] clause is included, processing continues with the highest level calling program.

---

*Caution*

Enclose each of these commands within an IF, ENDIF, or DO CASE, ENDCASE command set. Otherwise, the RETURN is encountered immediately.

# ROLLBACK

See **BEGIN TRANSACTION, END TRANSACTION**

# RUN/!

### *Purpose*

Performs operations that are available from the DOS prompt. For example, lists files on the disk, runs non-dBASE IV programs, changes directories, etc., without ending the dBASE IV session.

### *Reminder*

Although dBASE IV provides several dot prompt commands and Control Center submenu options, you are not limited to those few capabilities.

### *Command Syntax*

**RUN** *<DOS-commands>*

**!** *<DOS-commands>*

### *Procedures*

#### *From the Dot Prompt:*

Issue the RUN command to perform a program without leaving the dBASE IV session. For example, type `RUN CHKDSK B:` and press Enter to perform the DOS program called CHKDSK. Typing `! CD C:\dbase \deytol` changes the current directory to the **\DBASE \DEYTOL** subdirectory on drive C. Typing `RUN COMMAND` will call the DOS prompt. Type `Exit` and press Enter to return to dBASE IV.

#### *From the Control Center:*

1. Press F10 to access the menu line at the top of the screen. Select the Tools/DOS Utilities options. A window that contains file names, lengths, date, time, and space attributes appears on your screen.

2. Press F10 and open the DOS submenu. Select the
   Perform DOS Command option to issue and run a
   DOS command from the Control Center.
3. Select the Go to DOS option to suspend the dBASE
   IV session temporarily and present the DOS
   prompt. Issue and run the desired DOS commands.
   Then type EXIT and press Enter to return to the
   Control Center screen.

### Note

The ! command is a shorthand version of the RUN
command. Use either of these commands to run a DOS
command or another program from the dBASE IV dot
prompt.

### Caution

dBASE IV uses a large amount of memory. Many
programs cannot be run from dBASE IV with the RUN
command. Never RUN a program that will alter
memory. This may keep you from returning to dBASE
IV, possibly losing data. You will have to restart the
computer.

# SAVE

### Purpose

Saves memory variables, macros, and windows onto
disk.

### Reminder

dBASE IV assigns memory variable files a suffix of
.MEM, macro files a suffix of .KEY, and window files a
suffix of .WIN.

### Command Syntax

SAVE TO *<file-name>* [ALL LIKE/
EXCEPT *<skeleton>*]

**SAVE  MACROS  TO**  *<macro-file>*

**SAVE  WINDOW**  *<window-name-list>* /**ALL  TO**
  *<file-name>*

## *Procedures*

### *From the Dot Prompt:*
1. Create the memory variables, macros, and/or windows.
2. Use a SAVE command to save all the information on disk.

### *From the Control Center:*
1. Create the macros to be saved on disk.
2. Select the Save Library option from the Tools/ Macros submenu to write the current macros to the disk.

## *Notes*

Create memory variables with the = or STORE command and SAVE them to disk. Read saved variable files from disk with the RESTORE command.

Create windows with the DEFINE WINDOW command and SAVE them to disk. Read saved window files from disk with the RESTORE command.

## *Cautions*

If you restore a macro file that includes key assignments that already exist in memory, the new macro definition replaces the existing macro.

If you restore a memory variable, or window file, the ones in memory when the RESTORE command is encountered are overlaid unless you specify the ADDITIVE option.

# SCAN, ENDSCAN

### Purpose

Performs a set of command lines several times within a
program. For example, you can print a report of all
records in a datafile by writing a program with several
@...SAY commands.

### Reminders

Use the SCAN, ENDSCAN command set to perform a
loop. Each command set specifies at least one condition
that must be met for the loop to continue processing.

### Command Syntax

SCAN  [<scope>] [FOR <condition>] [WHILE
   <condition>]
       [<commands> ...]
       [LOOP]
       [EXIT]
ENDSCAN

### Procedures

#### From the Dot Prompt:

Include the SCAN, ENDSCAN command set rather than
the DO WHILE, ENDDO command set in a program.
Because the record pointer is moved automatically in
this command set, do not include the SKIP command:

```
use customer index customer
scan
  @ lncnt,01 say name
  @ lncnt,32 say phone_1
  lncnt = lncnt + 1
endscan
use
```

#### From the Control Center:

Looping is done automatically when you use selections
from the Queries, Forms, Reports, and Labels columns.

## Notes

The SCAN, ENDSCAN command set is similar to the
DO WHILE, ENDDO command set. However, SCAN,
ENDSCAN is always used to process a datafile. This
command set therefore handles the movement of the
record pointer and knows when it has reached the end of
the file.

The LOOP command immediately moves the record
pointer and processes the SCAN command line. Enclose
the LOOP command within a conditional IF, ENDIF
command set.

Use EXIT to end the looping activity immediately.
When this command is encountered, the program
continues running with the command following the
ENDSCAN line. Enclose the EXIT command within a
conditional IF, ENDIF command set.

## Cautions

If the condition specified by the SCAN command is
never met, the loop will continue forever. This situation
is called a hard loop. If the program runs longer than
you anticipate, verify that all loop conditions will end
eventually.

# SEEK

## Purpose

Has dBASE IV look through the data in the open file for
specific information. If, for example, you have a phone
directory of 2,000 records, SEEK tells dBASE IV to
find the name of Jerry P. Tuttle instead of you looking
through the datafile.

## Reminder

The search value for the SEEK command may be any
valid data type. A memory variable is not required but

gives programs more flexibility. For example, issue the command `SEEK A->NAME` to search the datafile for the value of the name provided by the datafile in work area 1.

## Command Syntax
**SEEK** <*expression*>

## Procedures
### From the Dot Prompt:
1. Open the datafile with its index file. For example, type `USE SUBSCRPT INDEX SUBSCRPT` and press Enter.
2. Issue a SEEK command with the expression to seek. For example, type `SEEK "SUSAN"` and press Enter.
3. When the dot prompt returns, use the DISPLAY command to view the records.
4. Create a memory variable (MKEY) that contains the search value ("SUSAN"). Then issue the SEEK MKEY command line to begin the search.

### From the Control Center:
1. Open the datafile and press F2 to view the data. Press Enter to move the bounce bar to the field you want to search.
2. Press F10 to access the menu at the top of the screen. Open the Go To submenu and select the Forward Search option and press Enter.
3. When asked for the search string, type it in the input area and press Enter.

## Notes
Uppercase and lowercase letters must be considered when providing search criteria. If the Control Panel's Match Capitalization option in the Settings submenu equals Yes, or the dot prompt's SET EXACT command is turned ON, all positions must match in case as well as length.

If you prefer to search the datafile for a value or its nearest value, use the SET NEAR ON environment command. If the specified value does not exist, dBASE IV returns the nearest match rather than an end-of-file condition.

## *Caution*

When using a search command in a program, use the EOF( ) or FOUND( ) functions in an IF command to determine whether the desired record was found during the search. Otherwise, you may be processing the wrong record.

# SELECT

## *Purpose*

Opens 1 to 10 datafiles, uses or changes the information, and closes the datafile to save any data changes on disk.

## *Reminders*

When you need to use several dBASE IV datafiles at the same time, each one must be opened in a separate work area. dBASE IV provides 10 work areas. Identify them by letters (a through j), numbers (1 though 10), or assigned alias names (similar to file or field names).

For example, the following command lines open two datafiles, assign alias names, and use fields from both datafiles.

```
SELECT 1
USE CUSTOMER INDEX CUSTOMER ALIAS
    CUSTFILE
SELECT 2
USE SALES INDEX SALES ALIAS
    SALESFILE
SELECT 1
DO WHILE .NOT. EOF( )
   DO WHILE CUSTFILE->CUSTNO =
       SALESFILE->CUSTNO .AND. .NOT.
          EOF( )
```

```
        MAMT = MAMT + B->TOT_SALES
    ENDDO
ENDDO
```

### Command Syntax

**SELECT** <*work-area-name/alias*>

### Procedures

#### From the Dot Prompt:

The proper syntax for the USE, CLOSE, and SELECT commands follows:

1.  Open the datafile with the USE command.
2.  Type `BROWSE` and press Enter. The Browse screen appears for viewing and editing. Press Esc to return to the dot prompt.
3.  Type `SELECT 2` and press Enter to access another work area. Then open another datafile.
4.  Type `BROWSE` and press Enter. The data on the screen is from the second datafile. Press Esc to return to the dot prompt.
5.  Type `CLOSE DATABASES` and press Enter to close all open datafiles.

#### From the Control Center:

The work areas for multiple datafiles are handled automatically when you create or open a database.

### Note

The CLOSE command lets you close any or all datafiles, indexes, procedures, and command files (programs).

### Caution

Work area 10 is automatically assigned when you use a catalog.

# SET

### Purpose

Changes the dBASE IV defaults for colors used on the screen, sets the number of decimal places for numbers, and performs other functions.

### Reminder

The dBASE IV environment is established when you begin the session. Each environment command is assigned a default setting unless otherwise specified by the CONFIG.DB file.

### Command Syntax

SET

### Procedures

#### From the Dot Prompt:

1. Type SET and press Enter. The Environment menu of options is displayed on your screen. Use the arrow keys to position the cursor on the desired option and press Enter to select it.

2. Continue to press Enter to change the setting in the menu. For example, position the bounce bar on the Date Order option, which is set to MDY (Month, Day, Year). Press Enter once, and the setting changes to DMY. A second press of the Enter key changes the setting to YMD. A third press of Enter returns you back to MDY.

3. When all environment options are set, press Esc to return to the dot prompt.

4. Use any of the SET commands from the dot prompt as in the following:

```
SET FUNCTION F4 TO "DIR *.*/P"
SET BELL OFF
SET DECIMAL TO 4
```

### *From the Control Center:*

1. Press F10 to access the menu line at the top of the Control Center.
2. Select the Tools/Settings/Options submenu lines from each window. The environment settings are listed in a window.
3. Use the arrow keys to position the bounce bar on the desired option and press Enter to select it for changes.
4. To change color selections also, use the Tools/Settings/Display submenu.
5. When all options are set, open the Exit submenu or press Esc to exit the Control Center.

*Notes*

Use the Display submenu to change the screen specifications.

Use the Keys submenu to assign commands to the function keys (F2 through F10, Ctrl-F1 through Ctrl-F10, and Shift-F1 through Shift-F9).

The Disk submenu includes two selections. The first selection changes the disk drive, and the second selection changes the subdirectory path.

Select the Files submenu to specify the Alternate, Device, Format, and Index files.

Unless the environment is specified in the CONFIG.DB file, dBASE IV uses the default values.

A list of SET commands follows. Default settings are shown in uppercase letters:

```
SET ALTERNATE on/OFF
SET ALTERNATE TO [<file-name> [ADDITIVE]]
SET AUTOSAVE on/OFF
SET BELL ON/off
SET BELL TO [<freq>,<duration>]
SET BLOCKSIZE TO <exp-N>
SET BORDER TO [SINGLE/DOUBLE/PANEL/
    NONE/<definition>]
SET CARRY on/OFF
```

SET CARRY TO [*<field-name-list>* [ADDITIVE]]
SET CATALOG on/OFF
SET CATALOG TO [*<file-name>*]
SET CENTURY on/OFF
SET CLOCK on/OFF
SET CLOCK TO [*<row>*,*<column>*]
SET COLOR ON/OFF
SET COLOR TO [[*<standard>*] [, [*<enhanced>*]
    [, [*<perimeter>*] [, [*<background>*]]]]]
SET COLOR OF NORMAL/MESSAGES/TITLES/
    BOXES/HIGHLIGHT/ALERT FIELDS TO
    [*<attribute>*]
SET CONFIRM on/OFF
SET CONSOLE ON/off
SET CURRENCY TO [*<expC>*]
SET CURRENCY LEFT/right
SET DATE AMERICAN/ansi/british/french/german/
    italian/japan/usa/mdy/dmy/ymd
SET DEBUG on/OFF
SET DECIMALS TO *<expN>*
SET DEFAULT TO *<drive>*[:]
SET DELETED on/OFF
SET DELIMITERS on/OFF
SET DELIMITERS TO *<expC>*/DEFAULT
SET DESIGN ON/off
SET DEVELOPMENT ON/off
SET DEVICE TO SCREEN/printer/file *<file-
    name>*
SET DISPLAY TO MONO/COLOR/EGA25/
    EGA43/MONO43
SET DOHISTORY on/OFF
SET ECHO on/OFF
SET ENCRYPTION on/OFF
SET ESCAPE ON/off
SET EXACT on/OFF
SET EXCLUSIVE on/OFF
SET FIELDS on/OFF
SET FIELDS TO [*<field-1>* [/R]/*<calculated-
    field-1>* ...] [,*<field-2>* [/R]/*<calculated-field-2>*...]
SET FIELDS TO ALL [LIKE/except *<skeleton>*]
SET FILTER TO [FILE *<file-name>*/?][*<condition>*]

SET FIXED on/OFF
SET FORMAT TO [<*format-file-name*>/?]
SET FULLPATH on/OFF
SET FUNCTION <*expN*>/<*expC*>/<*key label*> TO
    <*expC*>
SET HEADING ON/off
SET HELP ON/off
SET HISTORY ON/off
SET HISTORY TO <*expN*>
SET HOURS TO [12/24]
SET INDEX TO [<*index-file-name-list/multiple-
    file-name-list*>/? [ORDER [TAG] <*index-file-
    name*>/ <*multiple-file-name*> [OF <*multiple-file-
    name*>]]]
SET INSTRUCT ON/off
SET INTENSITY ON/off
SET LOCK ON/off
SET MARGIN TO <*expN*>
SET MARK TO [<*expC*>]
SET MEMOWIDTH TO <*expN*>
SET MENU ON/off
SET MESSAGE TO [<*expC*>]
SET NEAR on/OFF
SET ODOMETER TO <*expN*>
SET ORDER TO [<*expN*>]/[TAG<*file-name*>/
    <*multiple-index*>[OF <*multiple-index*>]]
SET PATH TO [<*path-list*>]
SET PAUSE on/OFF
SET POINT TO [<*expC*>]
SET PRECISION TO [<*expN*>]
SET PRINTER on/OFF
SET PRINTER TO <*DOS-device*>
SET PRINTER TO \\<*computer-name*>/<*printer-
    name*> = <*destination*>/\\SPOOLER/\\CAPTURE
SET PRINTER TO FILE <*file-name*>
SET PROCEDURE TO [<*procedure-file-name*>]
SET REFRESH TO <*expN*>
SET RELATION TO
SET RELATION TO <*expN-1*> INTO <*alias-1*>
    [<*expN-2*> INTO <*alias-2*> ...]]
SET REPROCESS TO <*expN*>

SET SAFETY ON/off
SET SCOREBOARD ON/off
SET SEPARATOR TO [*<expC>*]
SET SKIP TO [*<alias>* [,*<alias-2>* ...]]
SET SPACE ON/off
SET SQL on/OFF
SET STATUS ON/off
SET STEP on/OFF
SET TALK ON/off
SET TITLE ON/off
SET TRAP on/OFF
SET TYPEAHEAD TO *<expN>*
SET UNIQUE on/OFF
SET VIEW TO *<query-file-name>*/*<view-file-name>*/?
SET WINDOW OF MEMO TO *<window-name>*

# SHOW MENU

See **DEFINE MENU**.

# SHOW POPUP

See **DEFINE POPUP**.

# SKIP

### Purpose

Uses the SKIP command to move the current record pointer forward or backward in a database.

### Reminder

Think of a record pointer in a datafile as your finger moving through a phone directory. Your finger points to the name and phone number that you selected from the list.

*Command Syntax*
**SKIP** [*<expN>*] [IN *<alias>*]

*Procedures*

*From the Dot Prompt:*

1. Open a datafile with the USE command.
2. Type DISPLAY and press Enter. The first record in the datafile is listed on the screen.
3. Move down to the next record in the datafile by typing SKIP and pressing Enter. Display the record.
4. Move up two records in the file by typing SKIP -2 and pressing Enter. Verify the pointer movement by displaying the record.

*From the Control Center:*

1. Position the cursor on a file name in the Data column. Press F2 to display the data in a Browse screen.
2. Notice the middle section of the status line at the bottom of the screen. For example, 1 / 4 means that the pointer is positioned on record 1 of 4 in the datafile.
3. Press F10 to access the menu at the top of the screen. Select the Skip option from the Go To submenu. When asked for the number of records to skip, press 2 and press Enter.

*Note*

Use the INDEX or SORT command to put the data in other sequences. For example, enter the data as it is available. Then use the INDEX or SORT command to provide the desired sequence.

*Caution*

If the datafile contains four records and you issue the GO BOTTOM and SKIP commands, dBASE IV tells you that you have moved to record number 5. If you display the record, however, you find that it is blank and the status line shows EOF / 4.

# SORT

### Purpose
Orders the records to make finding information easy.

### Reminder
Determine the order or orders that you need to work properly with the data in the file.

### Command Syntax
**SORT TO** *<file-name>* **ON** *<field-1>* [/A] [/C] [/D] [,*<field-2>* [/A] [/C] [/D] ...] [ASCENDING/ DESCENDING] [*<scope>*] [FOR *<condition>*] [WHILE *<condition>*]

### Procedures

#### From the Dot Prompt:
1. Open the datafile. List the records and notice the sequence.
2. Issue the SORT TO command to create a datafile of sequenced records. For example, type `SORT TO STNAME ON STATE, NAME` and press Enter to create a sorted version of the data in a file called STNAME.
3. Open and list the data in the sorted file.

#### From the Control Center:
1. Open the datafile. Press Shift-F2 to display the data structure.
2. Select the Sort Database on Field List option from the Organize submenu.
3. A window opens for you to type the fields to be used for the sort. Type each name and specify it for ascending or descending order.
4. Press Enter to begin the sort. Another window opens. Type the file name and press Enter.

### Notes
If you need help with the field names, press Shift-F1 to open a window of fields included in the open datafile.

Use the arrow keys to move the bounce bar to the field and press Enter to select it.

Use the SORT command to sequence the data and save it on disk. The records are copied in the specified sequence to a new file. Therefore, the data is in the specified sequence, and the record numbers are sequential.

### Cautions

Before using the SORT command, consider the available disk space. Enough space must be available on the disk to accommodate two of the datafiles.

Do not sort on logical or memo fields.

# STORE

### Purpose

Creates a new memory variable or saves a value to an existing memory variable or array element.

### Reminders

The number of memory variables allowed is established through the MVBLKSIZE and MVMAXBLKS settings. The default settings follow:

```
MVBLKSIZE = 50
MVMAXBLKS = 10
```

A maximum of 500 memory variables is allowed by the default settings. An array uses one memory variable slot. Use the DECLARE command to create an array and the = or STORE command to provide values.

### Command Syntax

**STORE** *<expression>* **TO** *<memvar-list>/<array-element-list> <memvar>/<array-element>* = *<expression>*

### *Procedures*

#### *From the Dot Prompt:*

1. Copy the contents of a field to a memory variable with the STORE or = command. For example: STORE A->NAME TO MNAME is the same as MNAME = A->NAME.

2. Create other variables as in the following command lines:

```
MKEY = "Johnston"
MCUST = 301
MSWITCH = .T.
MDATE = CTOD("01/01/89")
MQTR[1] = "1st Qtr"
```

3. Display the current memory variables with the DISPLAY MEMORY command.

#### *From the Control Center:*

There is no equivalent capability through the submenus.

### *Notes*

The data type of a memory variable or array is established by the value stored in that memory variable or array.

dBASE IV provides several system memory variables for your use. Set and use any of these variables as you need. A brief description of each follows:

| | |
|---|---|
| _ALIGNMENT | specifies position of output "LEFT"/"center"/"right" |
| _BOX | specifies whether or not boxes print |
| _INDENT | specifies paragraph indention for the first line of each paragraph |
| _LMARGIN | defines the left margin for the screen and printer |
| _PADVANCE | specifies printer form, or line feeds |
| _PAGENO | specifies the number to be printed on the next page |
| _PBPAGE | specifies the first page of the next print job |

| | |
|---|---|
| _PCOLNO | specifies the column number of the print head |
| _PCOPIES | specifies the number of copies to be printed |
| _PDRIVER | provides the desired printer driver |
| _PECODE | provides the ending print control codes "BEFORE"/"after"/"both"/"none" |
| _PEJECT | specifies when a page eject must occur |
| _PEPAGE | specifies the page number to end print job |
| _PFORM | activates or identifies a print form file with all print settings |
| _PLENGTH | identifies the printed page length |
| _PLINENO | provides the current line number for the output device |
| _PLOFFSET | specifies page left offset for printed output |
| _PPITCH | provides printer pitch "pica"/"elite"/"condensed"/"DEFAULT" |
| _PQUALITY | provides print mode letter quality (.T.)/DRAFT QUALITY (.F.) |
| _PSCODE | specifies the starting print control codes |
| _PSPACING | sets the line spacing for printed output (1/2/3) |
| _PWAIT | specifies whether a pause between pages is desired |
| _RMARGIN | defines the right margin for the screen and printer |
| _TABS | sets the number of tabs for the word wrap editor, screen, printer |
| _WRAP | specifies whether word wrapping between margins is desired |

---

***Caution***

You easily can overlay an existing memory variable with a new value. If you need to save the existing value, save it in another memory variable.

# SUM

See **CALCULATE**

# SUSPEND

## *Purpose*

Suspends execution of a dBASE IV program. This command is valuable when debugging programs.

## *Reminder*

Use this command when you need to view variables, fields, and arrays. Then continue processing by issuing a RESUME command.

## *Command Syntax*
**SUSPEND**

## *Procedures*

### *From the Dot Prompt:*

1. Include the SUSPEND command in a program to stop the program temporarily. The dot prompt is available for you to display or change memory variables, datafile records, or any combination of information.

2. When you are ready to continue the program as though it had not been stopped, use the RESUME command in the program or from the dot prompt. The program continues running each command.

### *From the Control Center:*

This command is for programs only. Equivalent capabilities do not exist from the Control Center.

## *Note*

Include the SUSPEND command in an area of the program that you suspect is causing the problem. All memory variables, files, etc., are available after you process the SUSPEND command.

*Caution*

Remove all debugging commands before making the program available to the users.

# TEXT, ENDTEXT

*Purpose*

Prints, or displays a large block of information for the user without the user having to specify exact screen coordinates.

*Reminder*

Include the TEXT, ENDTEXT command set in a program. There are no equivalent menu options in the Control Center.

*Command Syntax*

**TEXT**
  *<text-characters>*
**ENDTEXT**

*Procedures*

*From the Dot Prompt:*

1. Include a block of information between the TEXT and ENDTEXT commands. For example, a program that includes the following command lines sends a banner page to the printer and advances to the next page break:

```
    set print on
       text
***********************************
*   This report lists information  *
*         from the customer        *
*      subscription datafile.      *
***********************************
       endtext
       eject
    set print off
```

2.  Remove the  SET PRINT command to stop the printing activity.

***From the Control Center:***

Draw a window on the screen and type the textual information in it. Also, creating an application provides an information window for the user.

### *Note*

When you use the TEXT command, use the ENDTEXT command to mark the end of the textual information. Otherwise, dBASE IV treats all command lines following the TEXT command as information for the user.

### *Caution*

If the information within the TEXT and ENDTEXT commands used on screen  is longer than 24 lines for the screen, the information will scroll past the user. To provide such a large block of text that the user can read, display a screenful of text, issue a WAIT command, and then provide the next TEXT, ENDTEXT information.

# TOTAL

### *Purpose*

Sums the values of numeric fields of the active database and creates a second database file to hold the results. The numeric fields in the new database have the totals for all records with the same key.

### *Reminders*

INDEX the original file before using the TOTAL command.

If the summed value is too large for a numeric field, dBASE IV will place asterisks in it. Use MODIFY STRUCTURE to provide numeric fields that are large enough for the number.

### Command Syntax

**TOTAL ON** *<key-field>* **TO** *<file-name>* [FIELDS *<field-list>*] [*<scope>*] [FOR *<condition>*] [WHILE *<condition>*]

### Procedures

#### From the Dot Prompt:

1. Open the database (it must contain at least one numeric field).
2. Create an index for the database.
3. Use the TOTAL command that specifies the key field used to create the index:

```
USE Invoice
INDEX ON Custno TO Invoice
TOTAL ON Custno TO Ninvoice
SELECT 2
USE Ninvoice
BROWSE
```

4. List the new datafile. Notice that one record is available for each customer with a sum of all invoice amounts.

### Caution

Verify that enough disk space is available for you to create the new datafile.

# ═══ **TYPE** ═══════════════

### Purpose

Displays the contents of a text file. This dBASE IV command differs from the DOS TYPE command by numbering the file and displaying it on the screen, to a printer, or to a new file.

### Reminders

Use TYPE for standard text files. Do not try to type databases or index files.

A dBASE IV program cannot contain a TYPE command to list itself.

## Command Syntax

**TYPE** *<file-name>* [NUMBER] [TO PRINTER/
TO FILE *<file-name>*]

## Procedures

### From the Dot Prompt:

Send a program or text file to the printer by issuing a command line such as `TYPE C:\INVOICE.PRG TO PRINTER` and pressing Enter. If the file exists in the root directory of drive C, and the printer is turned on, the document is sent to the printer.

### From the Control Center:

1. Press F10 to access the menu line at the top of the screen.
2. Select the Tools/DOS Utilities options. A window that contains file names, lengths, date, time, attributes, and space used appears on your screen.
3. Press F10 to access the menu line and select the Perform DOS Command option from the DOS submenu.
4. Issue the DOS TYPE command with the file name to type. For example, type the following:

```
TYPE INVOICE..PRG
```

## Notes

Use the TYPE command rather than the DOS TYPE command because you can send the information easily to the printer or another file.

You also can provide numbered file listings.

# UNLOCK

## *Purpose*

Releases file locks so that other users can access
records.

## *Reminder*

Identify the datafiles that must be available to several
users at the same time.

## *Command Syntax*

**UNLOCK**  [ALL/IN *<alias>*]

## *Procedures*

### *From the Dot Prompt:*

1. Open a database that has been converted to
   multiuser status.
2. Verify that you have the file locked with the ?
   FLOCK( ) command.
3. Make any desired changes to the database.
4. Free the database with the UNLOCK command.
5. Close the database.

### *From the Control Center:*

There is no similar capability available through the
Control Center submenus.

## *Note*

If the record is requested by more than one user, display
a message to the second user regarding the lockout.
Then let the user choose to wait for the record or
continue with other work.

# UPDATE

## *Purpose*

Uses data from another database to update fields in the
current database by matching records on a key field.

### Reminder
Both files used with the UPDATE command must be
indexed on the key field unless the RANDOM option is
specified.

### Command Syntax
**UPDATE ON** *<key-field>* **FROM** *<alias>*
    **REPLACE** *<field-1>* **WITH** *<expression-1>*
  [,*<field-2>* **WITH** *<expression-2>* ...] [RANDOM]

### Procedure
#### From the Dot Prompt:
1. Open both databases with their indexes.
2. Issue the UPDATE command. For example, update
   the Customer database with the total of all invoices
   as follows:

```
USE Customer
INDEX ON Custno TO Customer
REPLACE ALL Invtotal WITH 0
Select 2
USE Invoice
INDEX ON Custno TO Invoice
Select 1
UPDATE ON Custno FROM Invoice
REPLACE Invtotal with
Invoice->Totbill
LIST
```

#### From the Control Center:
1. Create a query to create a new datafile with the
   specified fields, sums, etc.
2. Select the Perform the Update Operation option
   from the Update submenu on the query screen.

### Note
If duplicate records are in the database being updated,
the first matching record is the only one replaced.

### *Cautions*

Do not specify a multifield key in the UPDATE command.

The UPDATE command changes the existing datafile. Make a copy of the datafile before issuing the UPDATE command while you are testing the programs.

# = USE

### *Purpose*

Opens 1 to 10 datafiles, uses or changes the information, and closes the datafiles to save any data changes on disk.

### *Reminder*

When you need to use several dBASE IV datafiles at the same time, each one must be opened in a separate work area. dBASE IV provides 10 work areas. Identify them by letters (a through j), numbers (1 though 10), or assigned alias names (similar to file or field names).

### *Command Syntax*

USE  [*<file-name>*/?] [IN *<work-area-number>*]
    [[INDEX *<index-file-list/multiple-file-list>*]
    [ORDER [TAG] *<index-file-name/multiple-file-tag>*
    [OF *<multiple-file-name>*]]] [ALIAS *<alias>*]
    [EXCLUSIVE] [NOUPDATE]

### *Procedures*

#### *From the Dot Prompt:*

1.  Issue the USE command with a datafile name to open it.
2.  Type DISPLAY STATUS. Press Enter to list environment information. Type SELECT 3.
3.  Open another file with its index. For example, type USE SUBSCRPT INDEX SUBSCRPT and press Enter.
4.  Type DISP STATUS. Press Enter to verify the indexed file.

5. Open the file with its index and assign an alias
   name. For example, type `USE SUBSCRPT`
   `INDEX SUBSCRPT ALIAS FILE1` and press
   Enter.
6. Type `CLOSE DATABASES`.

***From the Control Center:***

1. Position the bounce bar on the datafile name in the
   Data column. Press Enter twice to open the file.
2. When the Control Center returns to the screen,
   notice that the file name is displayed above the line
   in the Data column. This means that the file is open,
   and any changes made to the file need to be written
   on the disk.

***Note***

Work area 10 is automatically assigned when you use a
catalog.

***Caution***

Never turn off the machine while a datafile is in use.
Doing so is likely to damage the datafile so that you lose
much of the data you have entered.

# WAIT

***Purpose***

Causes processing to stop until any key is pressed by the
user.

***Reminder***

If a prompt is not specified with the WAIT command,
the default is "Press any key to continue."

***Command Syntax***

**WAIT** [<*prompt*>] [TO <*memvar*>]

### *Procedures*

#### *From the Dot Prompt:*

The WAIT command is used to stop processing and wait for user input. For example, the following command lines asks the user whether another record is to be added and waits for a response. The IF, ENDIF command set evaluates the response.

```
WAIT "Find another record? (Y/N) "
TO Mans
IF UPPER(Mans) = "N"
    RETURN
ENDIF
```

#### *From the Control Center:*

There is no equivalent capability from the submenus.

### *Note*

If the TO *<memvar>* option is included in the command line, a character memory variable is created automatically.

### *Caution*

This command does not provide control over the user input. Use the @..GET command to restrict the input.

### *Purpose*

Removes all records in a datafile.

### *Reminder*

Zap empties the datafile faster than the DELETE ALL and PACK commands.

### *Command Syntax*

ZAP

## *Procedures*

### *From the Dot Prompt:*

1. Open a datafile. Type ZAP and press Enter to remove all records from the database. If SET SAFETY is ON, you will have to press Y for Yes to delete all records.
2. Close the open datafile.

### *From the Control Center:*

1. Open a datafile and press F2 to use the Browse screen.
2. Press F10 for the menu and choose Records/Blank Record for each record in the datafile.

## Notes

ZAP reclaims disk space occupied by the deleted records.

dBASE IV asks permission to remove the records if the SET SAFETY command is turned on.

## *Caution*

When you issue this command from the dot prompt and SET SAFETY is on, dBASE IV asks whether you really want to zap all records in the datafile. The ZAP command in a program does not ask whether you want to zap all records in the open datafile. The task is performed immediately.

# dBASE IV Functions

Use any of the following special dBASE IV functions to perform a task or provide information. For example, the TRIM(mName) function makes the value of the mName memory variable appear as though it has no trailing blanks.

The dBASE IV function syntax follows:

**& <*character-string*> [.]**
    macro substitution

**ABS(<*expN*>)**
    absolute value

**ACCESS( )**
    access level of current user

**ACOS(<*expN*>)**
    angle size in radians of a cosine

**ALIAS([<*expN*>])**
    alias name of a work area

**ASC(<*expC*>)**
    character to ASCII decimal conversion

**ASIN(<*expN*>)**
    angle size in radians of a sine

**AT(<*expC*>, <*expC*>/<*memo*>)**
    substring search in a character or memo expression

**ATAN(<*expN*>)**
    angle size in radians of a tangent

**ATN2(<*expN-1*>, <*expN-2*>)**
    angle size in radians of a sine and cosine

**BAR( )**
    # of last selected prompt bar from the active popup

**BOF([<*alias*>])**
    beginning of file

**CALL(<*file-name*>, <*expC*>/<*memvar*>)**
    executes a LOADed binary program module

**CDOW(<*expD*>)**
    name of the day of the week

**CEILING(<*expN*>)**
    smallest integer > or = to specified value

**CHANGE( )**
    determine whether a record has been changed by a
    network user

**CHR(<*expN*>)**
    ASCII decimal to character conversion

**CMONTH(<*expD*>)**
    name of the month from a date

**COL( )**
     cursor column position on-screen
**COMPLETED( )**
     transaction completed or not
**COS(*<expN>*)**
     cosine value of angle in radians
**CTOD(*<expC>*)**
     character to date conversion
**DATE( )**
     system date (MM/DD/YY)
**DAY(*<expD>*)**
     day of month number
**DBF([*<alias>*])**
     name of the database in USE
**DELETED([*<alias>*])**
     record is marked for deletion or not
**DIFFERENCE(*<expC>*,*<expC>*)**
     difference between two SOUNDEX( ) codes
**DISKSPACE( )**
     number of free bytes on the default drive
**DMY(*<expD>*)**
     convert date to DD Month YY form
**DOW(*<expD>*)**
     day of week number
**DTOC(*<expD>*)**
     date to character conversion
**DTOR(*<expN>*)**
     degrees to radians conversion
**DTOS(*<expD>*)**
     date to character date conversion; for indexing
**EOF([*<alias>*])**
     end of file
**ERROR( )**
     error number of last error
**EXP(*<expN>*)**
     # from its natural log
**FIELD(*<expN>*[,*<alias>*] )**
     names of fields by numbers

**FILE**(*<expC>*)
> verifies the existence of a file

**FIXED**(*<expN>*)
> converts floating point # to binary coded decimal

**FKLABEL**(*<expN>*)
> name of function key from its number

**FKMAX**( )
> maximum # of programmable function keys

**FLOAT**(*<expN>*)
> converts binary coded decimal numbers to floating point

**FLOCK**([*<alias>*])
> locks a database file

**FLOOR**(*<expN>*)
> largest integer < or = to the specified value

**FOUND**([*<alias>*])
> logical result of a database search

**FV**(*<payment>*,*<rate>*,*<periods>*)
> future value of investment at fixed interest for a given
> time

**GETENV**(*<expC>*)
> returns DOS environment

**IIF**(*<condition>*, *<exp-1>*,*<exp-2>*)
> immediate if

**INKEY**( )
> decimal ASCII value of the last key pressed

**INT**(*<expN>*)
> conversion to integer by truncating decimals

**ISALPHA**(*<expC>*)
> first character is a letter or not

**ISCOLOR**( )
> checks hardware for color capability

**ISLOWER**(*<expC>*)
> first character is lowercase or not

**ISMARKED**([*<alias>*])
> database file is in transition or not

**ISUPPER**(*<expC>*)
> first character is uppercase or not

**KEY** ([*<multiple-index-file>*,] *<expN>* [,*<alias>*])

   key expression for the specified index file

**LASTKEY ( )**

   decimal ASCII value of key pressed to exit full-screen
   command

**LEFT** (*<expC>*/*<memo>*, *<expN>*)

   specified number of characters counting from left of
   string

**LEN** (*<expC>*/*<memo>*)

   number of characters in a specified string or a memo
   field

**LIKE** (*<pattern>*, *<expC>*)

   compares string using wild cards

**LINENO ( )**

   returns line number to be executed next in current
   program

**LKSYS** (n)

   returns the time, date, and log-in name for a locked file

**LOCK** ([*<expC-list>*] [,*<alias>*])

   locks datafile record in network system

**LOG** (*<expN>*)

   natural logarithm to base e

**LOG10** (*<expN>*)

   logarithm to base 10

**LOOKUP** (*<return-exp>*, *<look-for-exp>*, *<look-in-field>*)

   looks up record from another database file

**LOWER** (*<expC>*)

   converts uppercase letters to lowercase

**LTRIM** (*<expC>*)

   removes leading blanks from a character string

**LUPDATE** ([*<alias>*])

   last date of file update

**MAX** (*<expN-1>*/*<expD-1>*, *<expN-2>*/*<expD-2>*)

   greater of two values

**MDX** (*<expN>* [,*<alias>*])

   returns name of an open .MDX file

**MDY** (*<expD>*)

   converts the date format to month DD, YY

**MEMLINES** (*<memo-field-name>*)

    # of word-wrapped lines in memo field at current width

**MEMORY([0])**

    amount of RAM in kilobytes (optional zero does not affect result)

**MENU( )**

    name of the active menu

**MESSAGE( )**

    error message string of the last error

**MIN(*<exp-1>/<expD-1>*, *<exp-2>/<expD-2>*)**

    lesser of two values

**MLINE(*<memo-field-name>*, *<expN>*)**

    specifies a line of a memo field

**MOD(*<expN-1>*, *<expN-2>*)**

    modulus (remainder of numeric expression 1 by expression 2)

**MONTH(*<expD>*)**

    number of month from a date

**NDX(*<expN>*, [,*<alias>*])**

    returns name of an open .NDX file

**NETWORK( )**

    is dBASE IV installed and running on a network

**ORDER([*<alias>*])**

    name of primary order index file or .MDX tag

**OS( )**

    operating system in use

**PAD( )**

    selected prompt pad name of the active menu

**PAYMENT (*<principal>*, *<rate>*, *<periods>*)**

    periodic payment on a loan with fixed interest

**PCOL( )**

    printer column position

**PI( )**

    mathematical constant for the ratio of circumference to diameter

**POPUP( )**

    name of the active pop-up menu

**PRINTSTATUS( )**
    returns printer status

**PROGRAM( )**
    returns name of program being executed when an error
    occurred

**PROMPT( )**
    prompt of the last selected pop-up or menu option

**PROW( )**
    printer row position

**PV(*<payment>*, *<rate>*, *<periods>*)**
    present value of equal payments invested at fixed
    interest for a time frame

**RAND([*<expN>*])**
    random number generator

**READKEY( )**
    value of key pressed to exit full screen menu

**RECCOUNT ([*<alias>*])**
    # of records in the current database file

**RECNO ([*<alias>*])**
    current record # of selected datafile

**RECSIZE ([*<alias>*])**
    size of a record in selected datafile

**REPLICATE (*<expC>*,*<expN>*)**
    repeats a character expression a specified number of
    times

**RIGHT(*<expC>*, *<expN>*)**
    specified number of characters counting from right of
    string

**RLOCK([*<expC-list>*] [,*<alias>*])**
    locks at least one datafile record in network

**ROLLBACK( )**
    was the most recent rollback successful or not

**ROUND(*<expN-1>*, *<expN-2>*)**
    rounds the number in *<expN-1>* to *<expN-2>* decimal
    places

**ROW( )**
    row # of the current cursor position

**RTOD(<*expN*>)**
>    converts radians to degrees

**RTRIM(<*expC*>)**
>    removes trailing blanks (same as TRIM( ))

**SEEK(<*expC*> [,<*alias*>])**
>    searches indexed datafiles

**SELECT( )**
>    returns the number of the highest unused work area

**SET(<*expC*>)**
>    returns parameters of the SET ON/OFF commands

**SIGN(<*expN*>)**
>    mathematical sign of a number or expression

**SIN(<*expN*>)**
>    sine from an angle in radians

**SOUNDEX(<*expC*>)**
>    returns the four-character code used as an index to find
>    possible matches in sound-alike searches

**SPACE(<*expN*>)**
>    specifies a string made of blank spaces (254 maximum)

**SQRT(<*expN*>)**
>    square root of the specified number

**STR(<*expN*> [,<*length*>] [,<*decimal*>])**
>    number to character string conversion

**STUFF(<*exp-1*>,<*expN-1*>,<*expN-2*>,<*exp-2*>)**
>    replaces part of a character string or memo field with
>    another specified character string

**SUBSTR(<*expC*>,<*starting-positio*n> [,<*number-of-
characters*>])**
>    extracts a specified # or characters from a string or
>    memo field, counting from the right

**TAG([<*multiple-index-files*>,]<*expN*> [,<*alias*>])**
>    returns the tag name in a specified .mdx file

**TAN(<*expN*>)**
>    tangent from an angle in radians

**TIME( )**
>    system clock, HH:MM:SS

**TRANSFORM(<*exp*>,<*expC*>)**
>    picture formatting of character, logical, date, and
>    numeric data without using the @ commands

**TRIM(<*expC*>)**
    removes trailing blanks; same as RTRIM( )
**TYPE(<*expC*>)**
    returns an uppercase C, N, L, M, D, or U data types
**UPPER(<*expC*>)**
    converts lowercase letters to uppercase
**USER( )**
    returns the log-in name of the network user
**VAL(<*expC*>)**
    character to number conversion
**VARREAD( )**
    context-sensitive help
**VERSION( )**
    returns the dBASE IV version number in use
**YEAR(<*expD*>)**
    year from a date expression (YYYY)

# SQL Command Reference

The Structured Query Language (SQL) began in the mainframe and minicomputer environments. SQL is an advanced relational database language. The following commands are valid SQL commands:

**ALTER TABLE** <*table-name*> **ADD** (<*column-name*> <*data-type*>);
    add new columns to an existing table
**CLOSE** <*cursor-name*>;
    closes an SQL cursor
**CREATE DATABASE** [*path*] <*datafile*>;
    creates a directory and a set of SQL catalog tables for the new SQL datafile
**CREATE [UNIQUE] INDEX** <*index-name*> **ON** <*table*> (<*col-name*> [ASC/DESC] [, ...]);
    creates an index based on one or more columns in a table or view
**CREATE SYNONYM** <*synonym-name*> **FOR** <*table*>;
    defines an alternate name for a table or view

**CREATE TABLE** *<table-name>* (*<column-name> <data-type>*) [,...];
   creates a new table, defining the columns within that table

**CREATE VIEW** *<view-name>* **ON** *<table>* (*column-name>* {**ASC/DESC**] [,...]);
   creates a virtual table based on the columns defined in [*<column-list>*]other tables or views

**DBCHECK** [*<table-name>*];
   verfies that SQL catalog tables contain current SQL tables

**DBDEFINE** [*<.dbf-file>*];
   creates SQL catalog table entries for dBASE IV datafiles

**DECLARE** *<cursor-name>* **CURSOR FOR** *<***SELECT** *statement>* [**FOR UPDATE OF** *<column-list>*/ *<***ORDER BY** *clause>*];
   defines a cursor and an associated SELECT statement that specifies a result table for the cursor

**DELETE FROM** *<table-name>* [*<***WHERE** *clause>*];
   deletes specified rows from a table

**DELETE FROM** *<table-name>* **WHERE CURRENT OF** *<cursor-name>*;
   deletes row indentified by cursor

**DROP DATABASE** *<datafile-name>*;
   deletes an SQL datafile; removes all datafiles and index files from directory

**DROP INDEX** *<index-name>*;
   deletes an existing SQL index

**DROP SYNONYM** *<synonym-name>*
   deletes an SQL synonym name

**DROP TABLE** *<table-name>*
   deletes an SQL table

**DROP VIEW** *<view-name>*
   deletes an SQL view

**FETCH** *<cursor-name>* **INTO** *<variable-list>*;
   advances the cursor pointer and copies the values of the selected row into dBASE IV memory variables

**GRANT ALL [PRIVILEGES]/**<*privilege-list*> **ON [TABLE]** <*table-list*> **TO PUBLIC/**<*user-list*> **[WITH GRANT OPTION];**

grants user privileges for access and update of tables and views

**INSERT INTO** <*table-name*> [(<*column-list*>)] <*subselect*>;

**INSERT INTO** <*table-name*> [(<*column-list*>)] **VALUES** (<*value-list*>);

adds new rows to a table

**LOAD DATA FROM** [*path*] <*file-name*> **INTO TABLE** <*table-name*> **[[TYPE] SDF/DIF/ WKS/SYLK/FW2/ RPD/DBASEII/DELIMITED [WITH BLANK/ WITH** <*delimiter*>]];

imports data into an SQL table from a foreign file

**OPEN** <*cursor-name*>;

opens a cursor and positions the cursor before the first row in the result table

**REVOKE ALL [PRIVILEGES]/**<*privileges-list*> **ON [TABLE]** <*table-name*> **FROM PUBLIC/**<*user-list*>;

removes table access and update privileges

**ROLLBACK [WORK];**

restores a table to its previous contents prior to execution of commands in a BEGIN TRANSACTION, END TRANSACTION command set

**RUNSTATS [**<*table-name*>**];**

updates statistics in SQL catalog tables of the current datafile

**SELECT** <*clause*> **[INTO** <*clause*>**] FROM** <*clause*> **[WHERE** <*clause*>**] [GROUP BY** <*clause*>**] [HAVING** <*clause*>**] [UNION** *subselect*] **[ORDER BY** <*clause*>**/FOR UPDATE OF** <*clause*>**] [SAVE TO TEMP** <*clause*>**];**

displays data in rows from at least one table

**SHOW DATABASE;**

lists available SQL datafiles

**START DATABASE** <*datafile-name*>;

activates an SQL datafile

**STOP DATABASE;**
deactivates the currently active SQL datafile

**UNLOAD DATA TO** [*path*] *<file-name>* **FROM TABLE** *<table-name>* [[**TYPE**] **SDF/DIF/WQKS/ SYLK/FW2/RPD/DBASEII/DELIMITED** [**WITH BLANK/WITH** *<delimiter>*]];
exports data from an SQL table to a foreign file

**UPDATE** *<table-name>/<view-name>* **SET** *<column-name>* = *<expression>*... [**WHERE** *<search condition>*];

**UPDATE** *<table>* **SET** *<column-name>* = *<expression>*, ... **WHERE CURRENT OF** *<cursor-name>*;
changes the data in selected rows of a table

# SQL Functions

The following SQL functions are available through dBASE IV:

**AVG** ([**ALL/DISTINCT**] *<column-name>/<column-expression>*)
computes average value of a numeric column in selected rows

**COUNT** ([*\*/DISTINCT*] *<column-name>*)
counts the number of selected rows in a query

**MAX** ([**ALL/DISTINCT**]] *<column-expression>/<column-name>*)
returns the maximum value found in specified columns

**MIN** ([**ALL/DISTINCT**] *<column-name>/<column-expression>*)
returns the minimum value found in specified columns

**SUM** ([**ALL/DISTINCT**] *<column-name>/<column-expression>*)
sums the values of a numeric column in selected rows

# Index